◄｜150｜►
THEMATIC WRITING ACTIVITIES

Reproducible Reading-Writing Motivators for Students with
Diverse Interests and Learning Strengths

Tara McCarthy

SCHOLASTIC
PROFESSIONAL BOOKS

NEW YORK • TORONTO • LONDON • AUCKLAND • SYDNEY

*To my fourth-grade teacher
Ms. Helen Hultz and to all the children
in my writing workshop*

Cover design by Vincent Ceci
Interior design by Jacqueline Swensen
Interior illustrations by Steve Schindler

ISBN 0-590-49244-6

12 11 10 9 8 7 6 5 4 3 2 1   1 2 3 4 5 / 9

Printed in the U.S.A.

▲▲

CONTENTS

▼▼

▲▲

INTRODUCTION

▼▼▼

150 Thematic Writing Activities **is a set of 150 opportunities for your students to *practice* writing, with a minimum of supervision from you, and a maximum exposure for students to a wide array of genres, modes, and approaches. Students—individually, with partners, or with a small group—make their own choices about how they will respond in writing to a motivating story. On their own, they decide how to revise and share their work and then decide what they'll write about next.**

THE PRACTICE OF WRITING

Like any skill, writing needs to be practiced; and, as with any skill, practice *is* perfect, because practice involves *doing* and doing is learning. No matter what is the outcome, or product, the young writer learns through each of these writing "practices" something about what works and about what doesn't work, something about "how to do it" or about "how *not* to do it." She or he then applies this learning in the next practice session. Incrementally, or sometimes in big leaps, writing improves, as do the writer's thinking skills and sense of accomplishment and ease with this wonderful activity called *writing*.

Another way in which these writing practices are perfect for young people is that they happen in a playful arena: the motivating stories, or perks, are intriguing and lighthearted. They were designed this way because, for kids, the goal of an activity, whether it's skateboarding or softball, is often just the fun of doing it. Writing, too, can be a lot of fun, and the more fun and success students have with it on their own, the more easily and self-assuredly they'll undertake "serious" writing assignments.

PRACTICE ORGANIZED AROUND THEMES

The writing activities in this book do, however, also have a serious instructional objective, and that's why they are organized around themes.

As you know, theme-based learning proposes to integrate the curriculum by bringing concepts and skills from different subject areas to the exploration of a major topic, such as Patterns, or Fact and Fiction.

▶ One purpose of integrated or theme-based learning is to lead students to an enriched comprehension and appreciation of the concept expressed in the theme itself. In this book, for example, through writing activities organized around the theme *Great Jobs*, student writers explore many different, valuable ways of using talents and contributing to the general good.

▶ A second purpose of theme-based learning is to show students how to apply skills and understandings from different subject areas as they tackle a major problem in any one of them. For example, students who choose to write about the mythical kingdom of Atlantis (*Amazing Places*, Activity 17) are encouraged to do so by using what they know about geography, or about science fiction, or about civics and governmental organizations.

▶ The third, and perhaps most important, purpose of theme-based learning and integrated curriculums is to help students develop the higher-level thinking skills (analysis, synthesis, application, and evaluation) that are central to all genuine learning in any subject area and to use these thinking skills as they seek to understand any concept or to explore any situation, in or out of school. In other words, the overarching focus of integrated instruction and learning is not so much the theme itself or the application of discrete curricular-area understandings, but rather the holistic and creative use of universally useful thinking skills. In this book, for example, students who write about Weather Wizards (*Fact and Fiction*, Activity 34) become involved in analyzing and evaluating the veracity of sensory perceptions in general.

HOW THIS BOOK IS ORGANIZED

1. The writing activities are grouped under eight themes. Themes 1–7 have five writing activities. The eighth theme has seven writing activities. The activities are arranged in writing-process steps that make it easy for students to independently

---

Theme:
◀ AMAZING PLACES ▶
ACTIVITY 14

In the Land of the Brobs

▲▲▲

(A) In the book *Gulliver's Travels*, Gulliver goes to a land called Brobdingnag, where everyone and everything is giant size! For example, stairsteps are 6 feet high and serving dishes are 24 feet across. Glumdalclitch, the 9-year-old Brob girl who takes care of Gulliver, is 40 feet tall, and the other Brobs consider her small for her age. Adult Brobs are super big, of course. A Brob farmer picks Gulliver up and holds him 60 feet above the ground!

▼▼▼

RESPOND

(B) Make some estimates and measurements.

▶ List some things that are about as tall as Glumdalclitch.

_____

_____

▶ Measure *your* shoe. About how long are Glumdalclitch's shoes?

_____

CHOOSE A FORM FOR YOUR WRITING

(C)

___ I'll imagine I'm in Brobdingnag and write a **STORY** about my adventures there.

___ I'll write a **DESCRIPTION** of a classroom in Brobdingnag.

___ I'll **DESIGN AND WRITE A PAGE** for a book just the right size for Brob children.

◀ 42

(Activity 14 continued)

◀ **WRITE** ▶

Use the lines below to plan your story or description. Use art materials to make your book page.

(D)

_____

_____

_____

_____

_____

_____

_____

_____

_____

_____

◀ **A SUGGESTION FOR REVISING** ▶

(E) To help your audience understand giant sizes, include some exact measurements in your story or description. You can use *comparisons*, too. Example: "Glumdalclitch's puppy is about the size of an adult elephant." On the lines below, write some exact measurements or descriptions you can add to your draft.

_____

_____

_____

GOING ON

(F) *If you liked measuring giant sizes, you might enjoy writing about different ways of measuring other things (Activity 47).*

43 ▶

---

plan, carry out, revise, and share their own pieces of writing.

 A brief story or anecdote introduces students to an aspect of the theme.

B **RESPOND** gets your writers involved in the story by asking them to react to it with some specific ideas of their own.

C Students can choose, then check, any one of the three WRITING FORMS suggested; or they can think up an alternative writing form they'd rather use and write it after **CHOOSE A FORM FOR YOUR WRITING**.

D The **WRITE** lines on the page are usually sufficient for planning and drafting writing, however, extra reproducible pages with lines have been provided (pages 126-128). Visuals usually require other materials, and, as suggested in the lessons, some writers may prefer to do their drafts on a separate sheet of paper.

E The **SUGGESTION** may be for a way of revising, as here, or for a way of *sharing* a writing product.

F **GOING ON** encourages students to do some lateral thinking by using their ideas about this theme-activity to explore another theme. This is strictly an option, however; a lot of students will prefer writing further on the same theme.

2. Each theme unit concludes with a suggestion for designing and writing a **SPECIAL FORM**, through which students can **synthesize** the ideas they've gleaned from the writing activities and **elaborate** on them. For example, the theme-unit *Animals* concludes with suggestions and steps for making an illuminated manuscript; the **SPECIAL FORM** project that concludes the theme-unit *Great Jobs* gets students involved in writing newspaper display ads to "sell" their own special skills or aptitudes. The **SPECIAL FORM** activities are great opportunities for cooperative learning.

3. Preceding each theme unit, there is a page that provides a way to keep track of the writing forms individual students have chosen to do. Teachers can fill in the form themselves, or copy and post it for students to fill in.

HOW TO USE THIS BOOK

In your classroom, your students may already be writing in response to literature, writing across the curriculum, or reading and writing in special genres, such as mysteries, myths and legends, or journals and diaries. The activities in this book are designed to supplement, complement, and enrich your exisiting writing plans and program, not to supplant them.

There are two major ways to use the writing activities.

1. Use the individual pages to meet individual needs. With this procedure, you'll find the activities valuable as:

a. Brief warm-up activities for writing in particular genres. Scan the **Who's**

Doing What tracking sheet that precedes each unit to identify writing activities that focus on a genre your class is studying, such as short stories or news articles, and suggest that students try them.

b. Practice activities for writing in science, math, social studies. Again, scan **Who's Doing What** to find activities that encourage writing in different curricular areas.

c. Brief practices in responding to literature. The activity-pattern requires students to respond immediately to a short piece of writing and to choose a form for that response.

d. Opportunities for reluctant writers to become more comfortable with writing. The informal, high-interest nature of the motivating stories, the student's freedom to choose a writing form, and the clear and simple writing steps add up to a writing product that students have completed quickly and successfully. So, when a student complains that "there's nothing to write about" or that she or he "can't write," suggest that the student work with you or a partner to find a theme-based writing activity that tickles some interest and elicits some of the student's own ideas.

e. Opportunities for gung-ho, eager writers to experiment with many different writing forms. Even accomplished writers can fall into ruts, concentrating their talents in just a few familiar forms, such as short stories or reports. These writers will welcome the challenge of writing job descriptions, making glossaries, constructing survey forms, drawing and captioning charts or maps, or trying their hand at other writing forms that are relatively new to them. You might encourage these writers to try *two* of the writing-form choices suggested in an activity, or to flip through other writing activities to find another form they'd like to try with this one.

2. **Use the activities so that individual students and groups of students can take full advantage of the thematic organization.**

   a. Independently or with a writing partner, students can work through all the activities in a theme-unit that particularly interests them. They can then find a way to collate and organize their writing products to share and discuss with another student or another partner team that has chosen the same theme.

   b. The whole class can explore a theme as an exercise in critical thinking. With your students, you can choose a theme-unit for the class to explore together. In each activity, students can discuss the motivating story, compare their responses to it, develop criteria for the writing-forms suggested, share and evaluate their finished writing according to the criteria they've developed, discuss other ways in which the subject might be approached, and identify ways they can use what they've learned as they carry out other writing assignments.

c. A group can explore a theme as an exercise in evaluative thinking. A small group of students can choose a theme-unit to work on together. Suggest that as they do so they (a) focus on how the motivating stories develop different aspects of the theme; (b) discuss which stories they find most thought provoking; (c) discuss ways in which the stories relate to their own lives; (d) talk about ways in which their own writing helps them to understand the theme or story better.

d. Groups can synthesize their ideas about the theme in a cooperative learning project. (*See 2 under How This Book Is Organized.*) Individual students need not have done all the activities in a theme-unit to participate in creating the **SPECIAL FORM** that concludes the unit. To whatever extent the student has explored the theme, there is something he or she can bring to the culminating activity.

e. Groups can organize their writing for each theme into reference portfolios for the class. To get students thinking holistically, suggest that groups develop additional pages that cross-reference material about one theme to materials in another theme portfolio. For example, many of the activities in the *Word Play* unit can be cross-referenced to those in the *Puzzling It Out* unit. Students can begin their cross-referencing by referring to the **GOING ON** suggestion that concludes each activity.

Suggest that students also use the portfolios to get ideas for a curricular project to which they're assigned. For example, students assigned to write a social studies report on famous Americans can find start-up ideas in several of the thematic portfolios.

USE STUDENT INPUT TO ENRICH THE PROGRAM

150 Thematic Writing Activities is a book that will spark a multitude of ideas in your students. Encourage them to share their ideas by:

▶ **Suggesting writing forms that they don't find in the book.** Examples are greeting cards, package designs, contracts, book reports, postcards, movie reviews, and record jackets or audiotape enclosures. Ask students to add their ideas to a master list, keep it on display, and suggest that students try responding to the themes in these alternate ways from time to time.

▶ **Finding articles in periodicals, selections from literature, and sections in textbooks that relate to themes in this book.** Students can read the material aloud or make copies of it to post. Invite the class to discuss these "finds," tell how they add to their understanding of the theme, and suggest and carry out written responses to the material in different forms.

▶ **Thinking of new themes to discuss, explore, and write about.** Theme ideas may come from literature the class is enjoying together; from textbook topics; from local or national news events; from community or school celebrations and special events; or simply from a topic that fascinates students in general.

And don't forget to suggest in these brainstorming sessions the themes that interest *you*. Your enthusiasm for a theme can motivate your students to begin thinking and writing about it.

Encourage Students To Generate Ideas for Sharing Their Finished Work

Many of the theme-based writing activities include suggestions for sharing completed work. However, if you encourage students to discuss and carry out still other ways of sharing, they'll find more ways to integrate what they've learned and written into different curricular areas. In addition, individual students will be inspired to try writing forms their classmates have enjoyed.

To these ends, invite your students to help you make Suggestion Lists like the one that follows, which is based on the first theme-unit.

THEME: Animals
Suggestions for Sharing Completed Activities

Activity 1: *Super Star of the Sea*
▶ Read *stories* aloud. Make covers for them and put them on a reading-center table.
▶ Display and compare *maps*.
▶ Read *illustrated stories for young children* aloud to a group of kindergarteners or first-graders, and note audience reactions.

Activity 2: *Animal Fathers*
▶ Present the *science reports* aloud, including illustrations or chalk-talk pictures.
▶ Post *advice columns*. Ask classmates to add other questions animal parents might ask. Invite written answers.
▶ Invite writers to read the *diary entries* aloud, leaving out the name of the animal. Ask the audience to guess what the animal is.

Activity 3: *The Shopping-Mall Bear*
▶ Share *fantasy stories* in a tell-aloud session.
▶ Arrange *picture-and-caption stories* in a wrap-around-the-room mural.
▶ Invite a naturalist to read or listen to the *reports* and comment on them.

Activity 4: *Night Flyer*
▶ Read *persuasive paragraphs* aloud and get audience feedback about which facts best support writer's main idea.
▶ Compile *poems* in an anthology. Take turns reading one another's poems aloud.
▶ Work with classmates to decide if the *field-trip plans* are feasible.

Activity 5: *Mighty Mice*
▶ Collect *math word problems* in a folder and invite classmates to work them.
▶ Present *news reports* orally as a TV "Olympics Update."
▶ Work with classmates to dramatize the *comic strips*.

Theme:
◄ |ANIMALS| ►

Who's Doing What

ACTIVITY 1	Point-of-View Story	Map	Illustrated Story	Other Forms
ACTIVITY 2	Science Report	Advice Column	Diary Entry	Other Forms
ACTIVITY 3	Fantasy Story	Captions	Nature Report	Other Forms
ACTIVITY 4	Persuasive Paragraphs	Poem	Plans	Other Forms
ACTIVITY 5	Math Word Problems	News Report	Comic Strip	Other Forms

Superstar of the Sea

▲▲

A candy bar was named after him. His picture appeared on postcards. His life inspired a movie and many songs. He was Pelorus Jack, a 14-foot-long Risso's dolphin. For 24 years, Jack lived in the rough waters of Cook Strait, a 6-mile stretch that separates the two main islands of New Zealand. For some reason, Jack liked to guide steamships through the choppy, swirling waves. He met each ship, rubbed against the hull, then swam to the front and showed the ship's pilot the way through the dangerous French Pass.

Jack was so beloved that the New Zealand government passed a law that would punish anyone who harmed him. But in 1912, Jack disappeared, never to be seen again. A newspaper story mourned him this way: "If he is dead, more's the pity. If he has been slaughtered, more's the shame."

▼▼

◄| RESPOND |►

Stretch your imagination.

What motive, or reason, might Jack have had for guiding ships?

_____

_____

_____

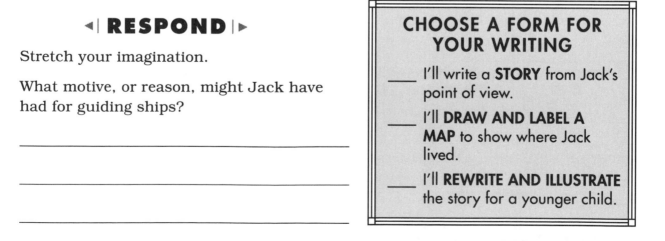

CHOOSE A FORM FOR YOUR WRITING

____ I'll write a **STORY** from Jack's point of view.

____ I'll **DRAW AND LABEL A MAP** to show where Jack lived.

____ I'll **REWRITE AND ILLUSTRATE** the story for a younger child.

(Activity 1 continued)

◄| WRITE |►

Use the lines below to plan your stories. Use art materials for your map or illustrations. Use the back of this sheet if necessary.

_____

_____

_____

_____

_____

_____

_____

_____

_____

_____

_____

_____

_____

_____

◄| A SUGGESTION FOR REVISING |►

How does your story sound when you read the first draft aloud? Use a tape recorder and find out. As you listen to your story, jot down any changes you want to make for the final version.

GOING ON

If you liked writing about an unusual dolphin, you might also enjoy writing about unusual dogs (Activity 23).

Animal Fathers

▲▲▲

The males of many kinds of animals take care of their young. Here are some examples:

After the pups are born, the male *wolf* stands guard outside the den and also brings food to them and their mother. As the pups grow, the father plays with them and teaches them how to find food.

Male *Emperor penguins* sit on the eggs to protect them from the cold. It takes about 60 days for the eggs to hatch, and during this entire time the father goes without food.

As the female *Siamese fighting fish* lays her eggs, the male catches them in his mouth, then carries them to a nest he's built. He guards the nest, then protects the young fish after they hatch.

▼▼▼

◄| RESPOND |►

How are male animals like the ones above like human fathers? How are they different?

_____

_____

_____

_____

_____

CHOOSE A FORM FOR YOUR WRITING

____ I'll do some research about one or more of these animals. Then I'll write a **SCIENCE REPORT** about the behavior of the fathers.

    seahorse   marmoset   rhea
       catfish   cockroach

____ I'll write an **ADVICE COLUMN** for animal fathers.

____ I'll write a **DIARY ENTRY** about the busy day of an animal dad.

◄|WRITE|►

Use the lines below to plan your writing.

_____

_____

_____

_____

_____

_____

_____

_____

_____

_____

_____

_____

◄|A SUGGESTION FOR REVISING|►

What important facts do you want your readers to learn from your report, column, or diary entry? List them below. Then check to make sure you've worked them into your writing.

_____

_____

_____

_____

GOING ON

If you liked describing animals, you might also enjoy writing their biographies (Activity 45).

_____

The Shopping-Mall Bear

▲▲

One day in May of 1992, a confused young black bear galloped through a busy shopping mall in a big New Jersey city. Some shoppers panicked, others kept their cool and called the cops. The state's two-member bear-response team arrived and tranquilized the bear. Then the team took it to *bear country*, a heavily wooded area in the northern part of the state, and set it loose: So when the bear would wake up, its surroundings would seem familiar.

But what was the bear doing in the mall in the first place? Animal specialists discussed two possibilities. The bear was a yearling, and may have been abandoned by its mother. Or perhaps an older, tougher male bear chased it out of the woods. Bewildered and lost, the youngster just kept wandering.

▼▼

◄ **RESPOND** ►

Suggest a couple of other reasons why a bear might wander into a shopping mall.

_____

_____

_____

CHOOSE A FORM FOR YOUR WRITING

____ I'll write a **FANTASY STORY** about a bear in a shopping mall.

____ I'll draw a picture story about the bear and write **CAPTIONS**.

____ I'll write a **NATURE REPORT** about bears in the area where I live.

◄ | WRITE | ►

Use the lines below to plan your story or report. Use art materials to design your picture story and plan your captions. Use the back of this sheet, if necessary.

_____

_____

_____

_____

_____

_____

_____

_____

_____

_____

_____

_____

_____

◄ | A SUGGESTION FOR REVISING | ►

Copy your draft on a word processor. Ask a partner to read it with you and make suggestions. Then work with your partner to move and add words and phrases until you're satisfied with your work.

GOING ON

If you liked writing about real-life animal adventures, you might also enjoy writing about fictitious ones (Activity 35).

Night Flyer

▲▲▲

For centuries, bats have had a bad reputation among people who don't know much about them. But among people who *do* know something about bats, bats seem marvelous and curious creatures. Here's what one poet had to say about a baby bat.

> *A bat is born*
> *Naked and blind and pale.*
> *His mother makes a pocket of her tail*
> *And catches him. He clings to her long fur*
> *By his thumbs and toes and teeth.*
> *And then the mother dances through the night*
> *Doubling and looping, soaring, somersaulting-*
> *Her baby hangs on underneath.*
> *All night, in happiness, she hunts and flies.*
> —RANDALL JARRELL

▼▼▼

◄| RESPOND |►

Jot your ideas below.

▶ Why do some people have *negative* views about bats?

_____

_____

_____

▶ How does the poet give a *positive* view about bats?

_____

_____

_____

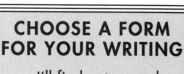

CHOOSE A FORM FOR YOUR WRITING

____ I'll find out several bat facts and write some **PARAGRAPHS TO PERSUADE** my audience why bats are OK.

____ I'll write a **POEM** about another animal that has a bad reputation.

____ I'll write some **PLANS** for a field trip I could take to observe real bats in action.

◄|WRITE|►

Use the lines below to write your draft.

_____

_____

_____

_____

_____

_____

_____

_____

_____

_____

_____

_____

_____

◄| SUGGESTIONS FOR ADDING TO YOUR WRITING|►

► If you've written factual paragraphs about bats, you might include some detailed drawings or diagrams to accompany them.

► Find all the descriptive words and phrases in your poem. Then draw an illustration that emphasizes these descriptions.

► Check your field trip plans to make sure they're in sequence.

GOING ON

If you liked writing about facts, you might also enjoy writing about superstitions (Activity 33).

Mighty Mice

▲▲

Mice are pretty strong for their size. In the wild, a mouse can jump many times its length. And the average house mouse, which weighs about one ounce, could probably lift its own weight.

So could mice have pulled Cinderella's coach? Not unless you could catch and harness about 495,000 of them! That's how many mice it would take to equal the power of one horse.

We use the word *horsepower* when we measure the power of motors or engines. One *horsepower* equals 33,000 foot-pounds. A foot-pound is the force needed to raise one pound at the rate of one foot per minute. Fifteen very strong house mice could raise a pound at about one foot per minute.

▼▼

◀ RESPOND ▶

Make some comparisons and estimates.

▶ Compared to a mouse, are you strong or weak? Why do you say so?

_____

_____

▶ How much *mousepower* equals one-half horsepower?

_____

_____

CHOOSE A FORM FOR YOUR WRITING

____ I'll write a **MATH WORD PROBLEM** about horsepower or mousepower.

____ I'll write a **NEWS REPORT** about mice, horses, and other animals competing in an Animal Olympics.

____ I'll draw a **COMIC STRIP** to tell a new story about Cinderella, her Fairy Godmother, and the mice.

◄| WRITE |►

Use the lines below to plan your math problem or new story. Use art materials and the back of this sheet to make your comic strip.

_____

_____

_____

_____

_____

_____

_____

_____

_____

◄| A SUGGESTION FOR REVISING |►

Check your work to make sure you've got your number-facts straight. A good way to do this is to exchange your first draft with a writing partner and read one another's work for accuracy. Then write ideas for revision on the lines below.

_____

_____

_____

_____

GOING ON

If you liked doing mouse math, you might also enjoy doing giant math (Activity 14).

A SPECIAL FORM:
An Illuminated Manuscript

▲▲

Illuminated manuscripts are written by hand in beautiful lettering. The writer weaves pictures and designs into some of the letters, and then *illuminates* them by using colors.

▼▼

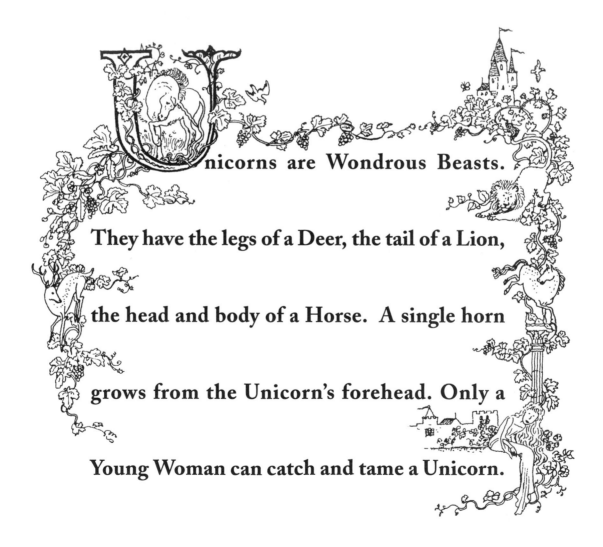

Unicorns are Wondrous Beasts.

They have the legs of a Deer, the tail of a Lion,

the head and body of a Horse. A single horn

grows from the Unicorn's forehead. Only a

Young Woman can catch and tame a Unicorn.

(Activity 6 continued))

Maybe you'd like to write an illuminated manuscript about your favorite animal. If so, follow the steps below. (If you want to practice first, illuminate the manuscript on the preceding page.)

1. On the lines below, write a draft of the sentences for your illuminated manuscript.

_____

_____

_____

_____

_____

_____

2. Revise and edit your draft. If you wish, ask a writing-partner to help you.

3. In your revised draft, circle the letters you'll decorate with pictures and colors.

4. Get the materials together you'll need for your final product:
- heavy drawing paper
- pencil
- crascr
- colored pencils, markers, or watercolor paints and brushes

5. Write and illuminate your manuscript. If you'd like, use the back of this sheet.

6. With some classmates, brainstorm ways to share your finished manuscripts. Write your best sharing-ideas below.

_____

_____

_____

_____

_____

Theme:
◄|GREAT JOBS|►

Who's Doing What

ACTIVITY 7	Interview Questions	Description	Pro and Con List	Other Forms
ACTIVITY 8	Persuasive Paragraphs	Narrative Paragraphs	Dialogue	Other Forms
ACTIVITY 9	Opinion Paragraphs	Job Description	Oral Story	Other Forms
ACTIVITY 10	Log	Math Word Problems	Short Story	Other Forms
ACTIVITY 11	Thank-you Note	Fiction Story	Biography Report	Other Forms

They Call Him Mr. Cyclone

▲▲

You take a look at Coney Island's towering roller coaster and hear all that screaming. It looks and sounds like fun, but is the Cyclone safe? As safe as possible, with Walter Williams on the job! About thirty years ago, he began his work as a coaster caretaker. Every morning he walks along the 3,000 feet of track, made up of nine drops and six turns. He checks bolts and wood and makes repairs. Once a day Williams rides the Cyclone, just to make sure the ride meets his high standards for smoothness. The ride's a thrill for the other passengers, but just all in a day's work for Williams.

▼▼

◀| RESPOND |▶

Think about job qualifications.

▶ What special skills does a coaster caretaker have to have?

_____

_____

_____

CHOOSE A FORM FOR YOUR WRITING

____ I'll write some questions I'd use in an **INTERVIEW** with Mr. Williams.

____ I'll write a **DESCRIPTION** of a ride on the Cyclone.

____ I'll imagine I'm Mr. Williams and **LIST THE PROS AND CONS** about my job.

◄|WRITE|►

Use the lines below to plan your questions, description, or list.

_____

_____

_____

_____

_____

_____

_____

_____

_____

_____

◄| A SUGGESTION FOR REVISING |►

Go over your draft with a writing partner to find ways to make your questions, description, or list *precise*. Take out vague or general words and replace them with *exact* words. On the lines below, write an example of a revised phrase or sentence your partner helped you develop.

_____

_____

_____

_____

GOING ON
If you liked writing about an unusual job, you might also enjoy writing about the job of being a king (Activity 37).

Be a Clown

▲▲▲▲▲▲▲▲▲▲▲▲▲▲▲▲▲▲▲▲▲▲▲▲▲▲▲▲▲▲▲▲▲▲▲▲▲▲▲

When the Big Apple Circus comes to Harbor Junior High School, it's not for entertainment. It's to teach students juggling, acrobatics, trapeze skills, stilt-walking, clowning, and other circus arts. The Circus Arts course is serious business! Students attend classes five days a week, after school and during the summer. Kids who sign up have to have a lot of patience and concentration. After much practice, they perform for parents and friends and entertain at street festivals. As their final exam, the student-stars put on their own circus performance. Some graduates want a circus career. Others simply want the experience of learning new skills and of accomplishing something through hard work. And the applause doesn't hurt, either!

▼▼▼▼▼▼▼▼▼▼▼▼▼▼▼▼▼▼▼▼▼▼▼▼▼▼▼▼▼▼▼▼▼▼▼▼▼▼▼

◄| RESPOND |►

Would you like to sign up for a Circus Arts course? Tell why or why not.

_____

_____

_____

_____

_____

CHOOSE A FORM FOR YOUR WRITING

____ I'll write a **PERSUASIVE PARAGRAPH** about why my school should have a Circus Arts course.

____ I'll write a **NARRATIVE PARAGRAPH** about a circus performance I've seen.

____ I'll draw a **PICTURE PANEL WITH DIALOGUE** about final-exam day for Circus Arts students.

(Activity 8 continued)

◄|WRITE|►

Use the lines below to plan your paragraphs. Use art materials and the back of this sheet to make your picture panel.

_____

_____

_____

_____

_____

_____

_____

_____

_____

_____

_____

_____

_____

_____

◄|A SUGGESTION FOR SHARING|►

Read your paragraphs or show your picture panel to a group of classmates. Ask them to comment on the parts they like best. Display everyone's final work on a Circus Arts bulletin board.

GOING ON

If you liked writing about difficult tests, you might also enjoy writing about a storytelling test (Activity 39).

Telling Stories for Fun and Profit

▲▲▲

People have been telling stories aloud for thousands of years. The setting used to be a cozy one, with the storyteller and a few listeners gathered around a fireplace or sitting on the porch. Nowadays, there are huge annual Storytelling Festivals in many parts of the country. The storytellers work for a fee or compete for cash prizes as hundreds of people listen.

To Ray Hicks, this seem like a sad development. Hicks, one of the most honored of today's storytellers, still tells his famous "Jack Tales" on his porch in Beech Mountain, North Carolina. He tells them the same way his family's been telling them for eight generations, kind of making them up and changing them as he goes along. Hicks doesn't approve of storytellers who get their stories out of books. And he doesn't think much of accepting money for storytelling, either. "Stories should be told for love and for wisdom," he says.

▼▼▼

◄| RESPOND |►

Do you think storytellers should accept money for stories they tell aloud? Explain your response.

_____

_____

_____

_____

CHOOSE A FORM FOR YOUR WRITING

____ I'll write my **OPINION:** Is storytelling a *job* if you don't get paid for it? I'll give reasons for my opinion.

____ I'll write a **JOB DESCRIPTION** of qualities a good storyteller needs.

____ I'll **MAKE UP A STORY ALOUD** and tape record it.

◄|WRITE|►

Use the lines below to plan your statement of opinion or your job description. If you're telling a story aloud, ask a couple of classmates to be your audience.

_____

_____

_____

_____

_____

_____

_____

_____

_____

_____

_____

_____

◄| SUGGESTIONS FOR SHARING |►

▶ If you wrote an opinion, get together with some other classmates who chose the same form. Compare and discuss your different ideas. Then make any revisions in your work that you think are necessary.

▶ Storytellers and writers of job descriptions can share their work and then talk about the differences between a story told on tape and a story told in person.

GOING ON

If you like passing stories along, you might like writing about a strange story you've heard (Activity 32).

Just Judy

▲▲

That's what she calls herself in her newspaper ads: Just Judy. She'll walk your dogs, feed your fish, do your grocery shopping, house-sit while you're away. She'll do your gardening, clean your files, bake cakes for your big party, return your books to the library, and then pick up the next books you want to read. As her ad says, "Got a job to do? Just ask Just Judy! Maybe it's something I'd like to help you with."

Judy charges a flat fee of $15 an hour. At first, she did all the jobs herself. Now that her business has grown, she hires other people to help her now and then. She pays her helpers part of the fifteen-dollar fee. The helper's share depends on how hard the job is and how long it takes to do. "I can't believe how successful this business is!" says Judy. "I never made this much money working in an office!"

▼▼

◄ RESPOND ►

Why do you think Judy's business is a success?

_____

_____

_____

_____

_____

_____

CHOOSE A FORM FOR YOUR WRITING

___ I'll imagine I'm Judy and write a **LOG** of one day's work.

___ I'll make up several **MATH WORD PROBLEMS** based on the hourly fees Judy pays her helpers for different jobs during an eight-hour day.

___ I'll make up and write a **STORY** about Judy's toughest job.

◄|WRITE|►

Use the lines below to plan your log, word problems, or story.

_____

_____

_____

_____

_____

_____

_____

_____

_____

_____

_____

_____

_____

◄|A SUGGESTION FOR REVISION|►

Logs, word problems, and stories make sense only when you've got all the steps in order. Work with a writing partner to check the sequence in your writing. Make any revisions you think are necessary. Then work with you classmates to find different ways of sharing your finished work.

GOING ON

If you liked writing about Judy's unusual business, you might also like writing about an unusual heroine (Activity 38).

Nobody Knows Who Did It!

▲▲

Who invented the light bulb? The telephone? The submarine? The computer? You can find the names in encyclopedias. You can even find out exactly who invented earmuffs, Frisbees, and yo-yo's! But a lot of things we use and depend on every day were invented or developed so long ago that we have no idea who the worker was.

For example, who took on the hard job of inventing and making button holes, boats, or shoestrings? What workers found out how to paint or how to make music? Who was the first person to make a pet out of a wild dog, to plant a flower garden, or to make a cradle to rock a baby in? These were great jobs, and we benefit from them. We just don't know to whom to give the credit!

▼▼

◄| RESPOND |►

Look around you. List some ordinary things whose inventors you wonder about. Examples are a table, a chair, a window.

_____

_____

_____

_____

_____

CHOOSE A FORM FOR YOUR WRITING

_____ I'll write a **THANK-YOU NOTE** to Ms. X or Mr. X to express my appreciation for an ordinary thing I use every day.

_____ I'll write a **FICTION STORY** about how some everyday object was invented.

_____ I'll find out who invented some modern machine or tool I use a lot and write a **REPORT** to share with my classmates.

◄ WRITE ►

Use the lines below to plan your writing.

_____

_____

_____

_____

_____

_____

_____

_____

_____

_____

_____

_____

_____

◄ A SUGGESTION FOR SHARING ►

Work with a group of your classmates to plan and present a Great Jobs ceremony. Read your written work aloud in a sequence that starts with the most modern inventions and ends with the oldest ones. Invite your audience to award "Work Well Done" prizes to the discoveries or inventions that they think are most useful.

GOING ON

If you liked writing about important ideas, you might also like writing about an unimportant idea (Activity 13).

✳

A SPECIAL FORM:
Newspaper Display Ads

▲▲▲

Most people who want a job look in the Help Wanted section of the newspaper to see what jobs are available. But *some* people try it the other way around: they buy display-ad space to tell about their special skills, and then sit back and wait for the phone to ring. To catch the newspaper readers' interest, these ads have to be peppy and a little unusual.

▼▼▼

CALL DR. WOOF!

**Got a sad dog? A fat dog?
A dog that wants a playmate?**

DR. WOOF will walk your dog.

DR. WOOF will talk to your dog.

DR. WOOF will introduce your dog to outdoor sports.

You'll notice a remarkable improvement in your dog's attitude and outlook on life!

Call: 555-FIDO

MEALS ON SKATE WHEELS

Quickie snacks and
Frozen dinners
We'll deliver, 'cause
We're winners!
Call in your list
(One bag, no more!)
And we'll skate it
To your door.

Call: 555-4657

Maybe you'd like to make a display ad to sell your own special skills. If so, follow the steps on the next page.

1. List some things you're really good at and that you enjoy doing.

2. Think about the needs of people and businesses in your community. Then, using your list from 1, circle the skills that you think you could use to fill one of those needs.

3. In the space below, write in pencil a draft of a newspaper display ad that will interest newspaper readers. Include a rough sketch of a picture for the ad.

4. Edit your ad by correcting spelling errors. Experiment with writing and with arranging words and pictures in eye-catching ways.

5. When your draft satisfies you, make a final copy of it on a sheet of drawing paper. Imagine this is going to be a full-color ad: use colored pencils, markers, or crayons to call attention to important points.

6. With your classmates, discuss ways to share your display ads.

   Here are some examples:

   ▶ Post your ads on a "Hire Me!" bulletin board.

   ▶ Arrange your ads under alphabetical headings for a classified telephone directory.

   ▶ Invite the advertising manager of your local newspaper to visit your classroom, study your ads, and tell about their strong points.

Theme:
◄│AMAZING PLACES│►

Who's Doing What

ACTIVITY 13	Labeled Diagram	Science Fiction	Letter	Other Forms
ACTIVITY 14	Fantasy Story	Description	Page Design	Other Forms
ACTIVITY 15	Letter	Journal Entry	Labeled Floor plan	Other Forms
ACTIVITY 16	History Report	Fantasy Story	Place-Name Chart	Other Forms
ACTIVITY 17	Map and Labels	Science Fiction	Rules and Laws	Other Forms

A Hollow Earth?

▲▲

Back in 1823, Captain John Symmes tried to get the United States Congress to give him money for an expedition to the center of the earth. Like thousands of Americans at that time, Symmes believed that the earth was made up of many hollow spheres, or concentric circles. Inside all of them, said Symmes, was warm, rich land filled with plants, animals, and possibly human beings. To reach these lands, all you had to do was cut through the ice at the North and South Poles and descend through huge holes. Though 25 congressmen voted to give Symmes the money, the majority voted *No.*

▼▼

◀| RESPOND |▶

Make an intelligent guess.

▶ Why did so many people believe the "Hollow Earth" theory?

_____

_____

_____

_____

CHOOSE A FORM FOR YOUR WRITING

____ I'll draw and **LABEL A DIAGRAM** to show what's really inside earth.

____ I'll write a **SCIENCE FICTION STORY** about a hollow earth.

____ I'll pretend I'm Captain Symmes and write a **LETTER** to a congressman telling how my expedition would help the world.

◄| WRITE |►

Use the lines below to plan your story or letter. Use art materials and the back of this sheet to make your diagram.

_____

_____

_____

_____

_____

_____

_____

_____

_____

◄| A SUGGESTION FOR SHARING |►

Get together with some classmates who chose the writing form you did. Read or show your work and then discuss it. What are some of the best ideas you shared? Jot them below in the lines provided.

_____

_____

_____

_____

_____

GOING ON

If you liked writing about a hollow earth, you might also enjoy writing about UFOs (Activity 31).

In the Land of the Brobs

▲▲

I n the book *Gulliver's Travels*, Gulliver goes to a land called Brobdingnag, where everyone and everything is giant size! For example, stairsteps are 6 feet high and serving dishes are 24 feet across. Glumdalclitch, the 9-year-old Brob girl who takes care of Gulliver, is 40 feet tall, and the other Brobs consider her small for her age. Adult Brobs are super big, of course. A Brob farmer picks Gulliver up and holds him 60 feet above the ground!

▼▼

◄| RESPOND |►

Make some estimates and measurements.

► List some things that are about as tall as Glumdalclitch.

_____

_____

_____

► Measure *your* shoe. About how long are Glumdalclitch's shoes?

_____

CHOOSE A FORM FOR YOUR WRITING

___ I'll imagine I'm in Brobdingnag and write a **STORY** about my adventures there.

___ I'll write a **DESCRIPTION** of a classroom in Brobdingnag.

___ I'll **DESIGN AND WRITE A PAGE** for a book just the right size for Brob children.

◄│ **WRITE** │►

Use the lines below to plan your story or description. Use art materials to make your book page.

_____

_____

_____

_____

_____

_____

_____

_____

_____

_____

◄│ **A SUGGESTION FOR REVISING** │►

To help your audience understand giant sizes, include some exact measurements in your story or description. You can use *comparisons*, too. Example: "Glumdalclitch's puppy is about the size of an adult elephant." On the lines below, write some exact measurements or descriptions you can add to your draft.

_____

_____

_____

_____

GOING ON

If you liked measuring giant sizes, you might enjoy writing about different ways of measuring other things (Activity 47).

The Weird World of Sarah Winchester

▲▲

There it stands, in San Jose, California. It has 160 rooms, 2,000 doors, 10,000 windows, 40 staircases, and 47 fireplaces. It was the home of the mysterious Sarah Winchester. Her father-in-law had invented the famous Winchester rifle, a weapon used to kill many people. Sarah felt sad about that and felt frightened when her husband and baby daughter died. By building this huge, weird house, Sarah hoped to confuse the evil spirits she imagined were after her.

For 38 years, 24 hours a day, workers built the house to conform to Sarah's directions. There are doors that open onto blank walls, secret peepholes, inside windows that never get light, and staircases that lead nowhere. Sarah's servants needed a map to find their way around! On and on the building went, stopping only when Sarah died. Today visitors find Winchester House amusing. But to Sarah it was a place to hide.

▼▼

◄| RESPOND |►

What's your reaction to Sarah?

_____

_____

_____

_____

_____

CHOOSE A FORM FOR YOUR WRITING

_____ I'll write a **LETTER** to Sarah to tell her how I feel about her fear and her house.

_____ I'll pretend I'm one of the workers and write a **JOURNAL ENTRY** about my day's building assignment in Winchester House.

_____ I'll **DRAW AND LABEL A FLOOR PLAN** of a house for Sarah.

(Activity 15 continued)

◄| WRITE |►

Use the lines below to plan your letter or journal entry. Use art materials and the back of this sheet to make your diagram.

_____

_____

_____

_____

_____

_____

_____

_____

_____

_____

_____

_____

◄| A SUGGESTION FOR SHARING |►

Get together with some classmates who chose the same form you did. Compare your work and talk about the best parts. Then make a folder for all of it, put the folder on a reading table, and invite other students to enjoy it.

GOING ON

If you liked writing about a fearful Sarah, you might like writing about a fearless Sarah (Activity 41).

Welcome to Death Valley

▲▲▲▲▲▲▲▲▲▲▲▲▲▲▲▲▲▲▲▲▲▲▲▲▲▲▲▲▲▲▲▲▲▲▲▲▲▲▲

It's pretty easy to figure out how some places got their names. For example, important things may have happened there! Many settlers who tried to cross the burning, rocky desert on their way to California just never made it. So the desert got the name Death Valley. Then there are other place-names that describe animals and plants that thrived there naturally, for example Grasshopper Flat, Lone Pine, Eagle Point, Wildcat Hollow, and Blueberry Hill. And there are lots of place-names that describe land forms and water, like Great Salt Lake, Black Canyon, Blue River, and Hat Mountain.

A great many American place-names come from American Indian languages or from European languages or from the names of individual people. Any map of the United States is scattered with place-names that reflect ethnic groups, events, and descriptions.

▼▼

◄ RESPOND ►

What's the name of your town or city? Where did the name come from?

_____

_____

_____

_____

_____

CHOOSE A FORM FOR YOUR WRITING

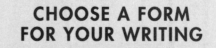

____ I'll write a short **HISTORY** of how my community got its name.

____ I'll find a really strange name on a U.S. map, like *Hot Coffee or Tar Pooch,* and write a **FANTASY STORY** about how the place got its name.

____ I'll make a **CHART** to show U.S. place-names that come from several different languages.

(Activity 16 continued)

◄|WRITE|►

Use the lines below to plan your history, story, or chart.

_____

_____

_____

_____

_____

_____

_____

_____

_____

_____

_____

_____

_____

GOING ON

If you liked writing about place-names, you might also enjoy writing about nicknames (Activity 46).

◄| A SUGGESTION FOR REVISING |►

Whether you've written a history, a story, or a chart, it should be in an order that's easy for a reader to follow. Work with a writing partner to make sure your writing has a sensible, easy-to-follow sequence. Then make any revisions you think are necessary.

A Perfect Land

▲▲

The ancient Greeks told the story thousands of years ago, and here is how the story goes: There was once a continent called *Atlantis.* People there lived in absolute peace. They had invented marvelous machines to do their day-to-day work, so that humans could devote themselves to the arts, to caring for all living things, and to friendship. Then slowly, the people grew greedy, and their rulers grew cruel and power-hungry. Before long, like some kind of punishment, huge volcanoes and earthquakes destroyed Atlantis, and the continent sank beneath the sea, never to be seen again. Atlantis is just one of the many perfect lands that people everywhere tell about in myths and legends.

▼▼

◀| RESPOND |▶

Why do you think legends about perfect lands have been remembered and retold down through the centuries?

_____

_____

_____

_____

_____

_____

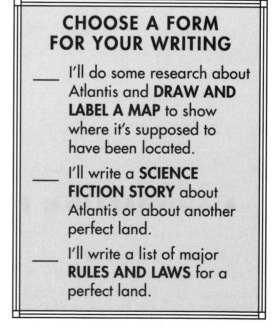

CHOOSE A FORM FOR YOUR WRITING

____ I'll do some research about Atlantis and **DRAW AND LABEL A MAP** to show where it's supposed to have been located.

____ I'll write a **SCIENCE FICTION STORY** about Atlantis or about another perfect land.

____ I'll write a list of major **RULES AND LAWS** for a perfect land.

◄ | **WRITE** | ►

Use the lines below to plan your science fiction story or your list of rules and laws. Use art materials and the back of this sheet to make your map.

_____

_____

_____

_____

_____

_____

_____

_____

_____

_____

_____

_____

_____

◄ | **A SUGGESTION FOR SHARING** | ►

Get together with some classmates who chose the same writing form you did. Compare your results. Make a chart or list to show *agreements* and *disagreements*. Then discuss your disagreements and find ways to support your own findings or opinions.

GOING ON

If you liked writing about long ago beliefs, you might also enjoy writing about mystery creatures (Activity 49).

✳

A SPECIAL FORM:
Travel Brochures

▲▲▲▲▲▲▲▲▲▲▲▲▲▲▲▲▲▲▲▲▲▲▲▲▲▲▲▲ ▲▲▲▲▲▲

A travel brochure is part advertisement and part nitty-gritty information. Usually there are four pages. The first page, like the one shown, is designed to get travelers excited about going to a particular place. The next three pages of a brochure give details about the trip, such as:

When does it start and end?

How much does it cost?

How do travelers get to the starting point?

How many travelers are in the group?

What is the schedule for each day?

Where will travelers eat and sleep?

What are the qualifications of the trip guides?

THE AMAZON RAIN FOREST IS CALLING YOU!

Come see the rushing rivers, the magnificent plants and animals!

Sign up with Wilderness Forever Tours for your own guided 8-day journey through this fragile and beautiful ecosystem. *MORE →*

All the pages of a travel brochure usually have exciting pictures and maps that keep readers' interest high. On the last page, there's often a form to fill out and mail if you want more information or if you want to sign up for the trip.

▼▼▼▼▼▼▼▼▼▼▼▼▼▼▼▼▼▼▼▼▼▼▼▼▼▼▼▼▼▼▼▼▼▼▼▼▼

Maybe you'd like to design and make a travel brochure about an amazing place. The place can be real, like Death Valley, or imaginary, like the Land of the Brobs or Atlantis. Use the steps on the next page to help you plan your travel brochure.

(Activity 18 continued)

1. Write the name of the place your brochure tells about.

2. Briefly list reasons why travelers would enjoy this place.

3. On the lines below, make notes about the information and pictures you'll use on the four pages.

Page 1

_____

_____

_____

Page 2

_____

_____

_____

Page 3

_____

_____

Page 4

_____

_____

4. Fold a piece of paper in half and use it as a rough-draft worksheet for the words and pictures in your travel folder.

5. With a partner or group of classmates, check over your draft. Does it include the information listed on the separate page?

6. Collect the art materials you'll need to make your final product: good sturdy paper, drawing and coloring tools like crayons and markers, and a pen for writing the words. Make your brochure.

7. With your classmates, brainstorm some ways to share your travel brochures. Write your sharing ideas on the lines below.

_____

_____

_____

_____

_____

Theme:
◄|WORD PLAY|►

Who's Doing What

ACTIVITY 19	Word and Phrase List	Definitions	Play	Other Forms
ACTIVITY 20	Journal	Poem	Book for Younger Children	Other Forms
ACTIVITY 21	Poem	Survey Questions	TV Script	Other Forms
ACTIVITY 22	Anagram List	Humorous Poem	Game	Other Forms
ACTIVITY 23	Personal Experience Story	Research Report	Fantasy Story	Other Forms

Words That Mean Their Opposites

▲▲▲▲▲▲▲▲▲▲▲▲▲▲▲▲▲▲▲▲▲▲▲▲▲▲▲▲▲▲▲▲▲▲▲▲▲▲▲

The English language can be peculiar! A word or phrase that means one thing can also mean its very opposite. Here are some examples:

1. The furnace *gave out* a lot of heat,
     but then it *gave out.*
   Give out can mean "produce,"
     and also "stop producing."

2. If you *bolt* the barn door,
     the horse won't *bolt.*
   Bolt can mean "fasten in place,"
     and also "run away."

3. When I *left* the room,
     five people were *left.*
   Left can mean "departed,"
     and also "remained."

▼▼▼▼▼▼▼▼▼▼▼▼▼▼▼▼▼▼▼▼▼▼▼▼▼▼▼▼▼▼▼▼▼▼▼▼▼▼▼

◀ | RESPOND | ▶

▶ Imagine yourself learning English as a new language. What's going to be hard about it?

_____

_____

▶ How will you get help?

_____

_____

(Activity 19 continued)

CHOOSE A FORM FOR YOUR WRITING

____ I'll make a **WORD-AND-PHRASE LIST** of English expressions I think a newcomer should learn.

____ I'll use a dictionary to find and **WRITE OPPOSITE DEFINITIONS** for *clip*, *fast*, *dust*, *screen*, and *trim*.

____ I'll write a short, funny **PLAY** in which the characters get mixed up over word meanings.

◄ |WRITE|►

Use the lines below to plan your list, definitions, or play.

_____

_____

_____

_____

_____

_____

_____

_____

_____

_____

_____

_____

_____

GOING ON

If you liked writing about word mix-ups, you might also enjoy writing about riddles (Activity 43).

◄| A SUGGESTION FOR SHARING AND REVISING |►

Get together with two classmates who chose two writing forms different from the one you chose. Discuss different words and phrases the three of you used. Revise your writing by adding ideas you got from your discussion.

Sorry To Hear About Your Graphophobia!

▲▲

That's what you might write on a sympathy note to a friend who has a *fear of writing*. *Phobia* is from an old Latin word meaning "an intense, constant fear." *Grapho* is from the Latin word meaning "write." By combining *phobia* with other Latin words, we make words naming other fears, such as:

amanthophobia: fear of dust; *bibliophobia:* fear of books;

chromophobia: fear of colors; *hodophobia:* fear of travel.

The fears listed above are rare and may sound silly. But almost everyone's afraid of something, and some fears are common, such as:

claustrophobia: fear of small, enclosed spaces;

lygophobia: fear of the dark; *demophobia:* fear of crowds.

▼▼▼

◀| RESPOND |▶

What are *you* afraid of? (If you're afraid of writing down your fear, you have *phobophobia*!)

_____

_____

_____

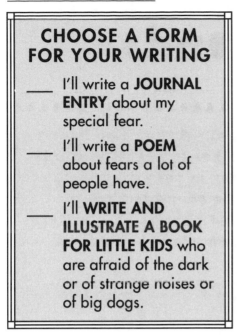

CHOOSE A FORM FOR YOUR WRITING

____ I'll write a **JOURNAL ENTRY** about my special fear.

____ I'll write a **POEM** about fears a lot of people have.

____ I'll **WRITE AND ILLUSTRATE A BOOK FOR LITTLE KIDS** who are afraid of the dark or of strange noises or of big dogs.

◄| WRITE |►

Use the lines below to plan your journal entry or poem. Use writing and art materials to plan your book for little children.

_____

_____

_____

_____

_____

_____

_____

_____

_____

◄| A SUGGESTION FOR REVISING |►

It's not always easy to write about fears. Writers often find themselves using the same words over and over again, like *scared*, *afraid*, and *frightened*. Use a thesaurus or a dictionary to find some other great words for describing fearful feelings. How about *appalled*, *trembling*, or *horrified*, for instance? On the lines below, write some other words you find can communicate the feeling of fear. Use some of these words to replace ones you've overused in your rough draft.

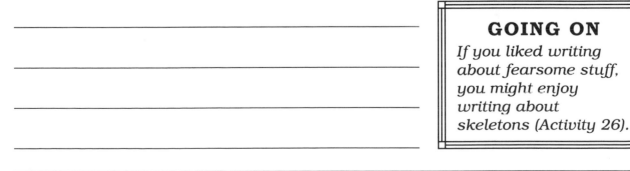

_____

_____

_____

_____

GOING ON

If you liked writing about fearsome stuff, you might enjoy writing about skeletons (Activity 26).

Beautiful Sounds

▲▲

Words have meanings, but when you say them aloud they also have a sound. Writers sometimes challenge one another to beautiful-words-and-phrases contests. These contests aren't as easy as they may seem at first, because you have to pay attention only to the *sound* and try to forget the *meaning*. Here are some of the words and phrases that writers have chosen as Very Beautiful. You have to say them aloud to find out whether you agree.

murmur	hush	bobolink	fawn	marigold
mist	lullaby	lilac	memory	harbors
home	nevermore	fair	mouse	cobblestone

▼▼

◄| RESPOND |►

Circle the three words above that you think have the most beautiful sound. Then write six other words, not from the list above, that you think sound beautiful. Use a dictionary if you want to.

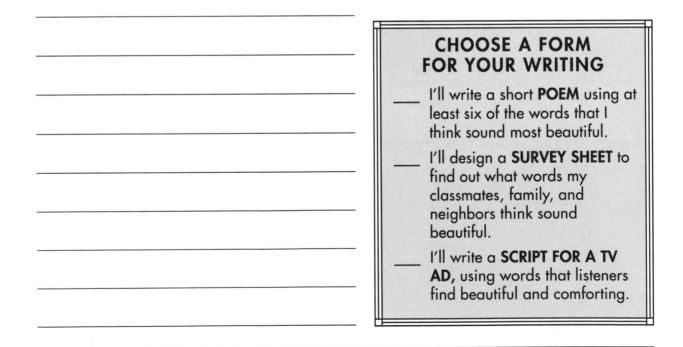

CHOOSE A FORM FOR YOUR WRITING

____ I'll write a short **POEM** using at least six of the words that I think sound most beautiful.

____ I'll design a **SURVEY SHEET** to find out what words my classmates, family, and neighbors think sound beautiful.

____ I'll write a **SCRIPT FOR A TV AD,** using words that listeners find beautiful and comforting.

(Activity 21 continued)

◄|WRITE|►

Use the lines below to plan your poem, survey sheet, or TV script.

_____

_____

_____

_____

_____

_____

_____

_____

_____

_____

_____

_____

_____

◄| A SUGGESTION FOR SHARING |►

▶ If you wrote a poem or TV ad, read your work aloud to your classmates. Challenge them to listen to identify the "sounds-beautiful" words you chose.

▶ If you made a "sounds-beautiful" survey, compare the results with a classmate who chose the same writing form. Discuss how you could use "beautiful words" to convince people to join you in a cause or program you have in mind.

GOING ON
If you liked playing with words and sounds, you might also like using them to describe a bat (Activity 4).

Word Games: Anagrams

▲▲

An *anagram* is the rearrangement of letters in a word to make a new word or words. Figure out why the boxed words in the sentences that follow are anagrams:

N O W her O W N team's W O N.

Her T E A M is T A M E.

Let's E A T and have T E A.

She's a S T A R at A R T S.

Anagrams are favorites for writers who like to play with words. Here's some anagram fun with the word stop.

The sign says <u>Stop</u>! Put down your <u>pots</u>!

One has a <u>spot</u>, and two have <u>tops</u>.

▼▼

◄| RESPOND |►

► Change *slip* to something you have on your face.

_____

► Change *south* to a very loud sound.

_____

► Change *live* to the opposite of good.

_____

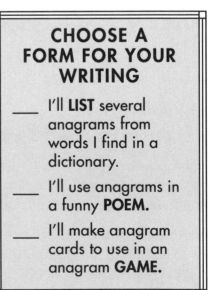

CHOOSE A FORM FOR YOUR WRITING

___ I'll **LIST** several anagrams from words I find in a dictionary.

___ I'll use anagrams in a funny **POEM.**

___ I'll make anagram cards to use in an anagram **GAME.**

◄|WRITE|►

Use the lines below to make your list, plan your poem, or design your game.

_____

_____

_____

_____

_____

_____

_____

_____

_____

_____

_____

◄| SUGGESTIONS FOR SHARING |►

► If you made an anagram game, write down the rules that players should follow. Then test the rules with a partner. Revise any rules that don't work. Then share your game with some classmates.

► If you made an anagram list, work with a partner to make sure your anagrams are accurate. Then display your anagrams on a bulletin board.

► If you wrote an anagram poem, challenge your classmates in two ways:

1) Ask them to identify the anagrams when you read the poem aloud.

2) Write and display a neat copy of your poem. Ask classmates to read your poem and find the anagrams.

GOING ON
If you like playing with words, go on to some word play in Activity 29.

Whistle Talk

▲▲

Sheep are famous for their scattered ways. They scare easily, run off in different directions, and tend to get lost. To keep the sheep together and to move them in the right direction, the herder and his or her dog work as a team. The dog keeps its eyes on the flock and listens for directions from the herder. The directions to the dog are given in the form of whistles. There are four basic whistle signals. One kind means "walk up toward the sheep." Another kind means "stop moving" (lie down or stand still). The third and fourth kinds of whistles tell the dog to move to the left or to the right around the flock. The whistle language is efficient because the dog can hear the directions when it's out of sight of the herder.

▼▼

◄| RESPOND |►

Why do you think sheepdogs understand the whistles?

_____

_____

_____

_____

CHOOSE A FORM FOR YOUR WRITING

____ I'll write a true **PERSONAL EXPERIENCE STORY** about communicating with an animal.

____ I'll do some research about sheepdogs and their training and write a **REPORT** on the subject.

____ I'll write a **FANTASY STORY** in which dogs learn to speak.

◄ **WRITE** ►

Use the lines below to plan your story or report.

_____

_____

_____

_____

_____

_____

_____

_____

_____

_____

_____

◄ **A SUGGESTION FOR REVISING** ►

A personal story, a report, and a fantasy story all have to be told in an understandable sequence, or order. Ask a partner to check the sequence in your writing to make sure it's clear to the reader. Then make any revisions you think are necessary. Maybe you'll need to add a step. If so, jot some notes about the step you'll add.

_____

_____

_____

_____

GOING ON

If you liked writing about animal communication, you might also enjoy writing about animal parents (Activity 2).

✳

A SPECIAL FORM:
A GLOSSARY

▲▲▲

A *glossary* **is an alphabetical list of words and definitions on a specific topic. For example, a book about dogs might have a glossary in the back listing special words and terms that refer to dogs. A book about ghosts might have a Ghostly Glossary of words and terms we use when discussing ghosts. But you don't have to write a book to make a glossary. You can make your own glossary on almost any subject at all. You can even make up a glossary of words you make up! Here's an example:**

◀ **bumbledacious:** *being rather clumsy*

catmew: *a complaining sound*

drissy: *a soft, warm rain*

glump: *to walk in a sad way* ▶

jellyism: *a tendency to change your mind a lot*

▼▼▼

Maybe you'd like to try making a glossary of your own. As in many glossaries, you can draw pictures to illustrate some of the entries. Some glossary categories are listed below. Check a category you want to use, or make up a category of your own.

_____ science words   _____ math words   _____ social studies words

_____ weather words   _____ words about school   _____ made-up words

_____ names of people in books I've enjoyed

_____ words about a special group of animals

I've thought of another category for my glossary. It's _____.

Use the steps on the next page to help you plan your glossary.

1. Write ten words you want to define in your glossary. List the words in alphabetical order.

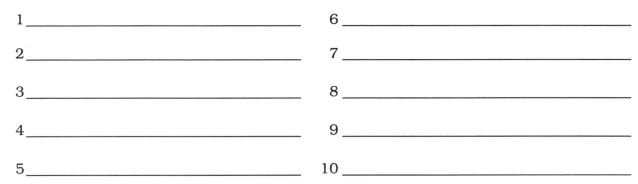

1 _____   6 _____

2 _____   7 _____

3 _____   8 _____

4 _____   9 _____

5 _____   10 _____

2. On a separate sheet of paper, make a rough draft of your glossary by writing the ten words and their definitions.

3. Go over your draft with a partner. If your glossary is about words that already exist, such as science words or math words, work with your partner and a dictionary to make sure you've got the definitions right. If your glossary is a list of words you've made up, discuss with your partner how each word describes something in a new way. Also ask your partner which glossary words need an illustration to make the definition clear. Write your partner's best suggestions on the lines below.

_____

_____

_____

4. Make a final copy of your glossary and give it a title, such as "Absolutely Necessary Words If You Want to Pass the Math Test," or "Funny New Words for Far-Out Word Fanatics."

5. With your classmates, brainstorm some ways to share your glossaries. Write the sharing ideas you like best below.

_____

_____

_____

_____

Theme:
◄|PATTERNS AND SHAPES|►

Who's Doing What

ACTIVITY 25	Captions	Fantasy Story	Descriptive Paragraph	Other Forms
ACTIVITY 26	Newspaper Story	Poem	Labeled Drawing	Other Forms
ACTIVITY 27	Explanatory Paragraphs	Rebus Story	Coat-of Arms & Motto	Other Forms
ACTIVITY 28	Science Report	Explaining a Strategy	Poem	Other Forms
ACTIVITY 29	Explanation	Glossary	Fable	Other Forms

Quizzical Quilts

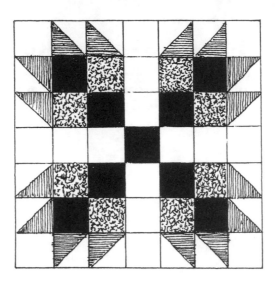

▲▲

A quilt is something to keep you warm. But in olden days, a quilt pattern also told something about the environment of the people who made the quilt. The quilt in the picture is called the *bear claw.* Back in those times, there were still many bears around, so quilters found inspiration in the pawprints these animals left in fields and forests. Long-ago quilters also made wedding-ring designs, spring-flower designs, and designs based on the stars they saw gleaming in the clear night sky. Quilters today might develop designs based on modern-day life.

▼▼

◄| RESPOND |►

Imagine that you're designing a quilt for today. Think of a modern-day pattern you might repeat in each quilt square.

CHOOSE A FORM FOR YOUR WRITING

_____ I'll draw a rectangle to represent a quilt and divide it into 12 equal sections. Then I'll **WRITE A CAPTION** to tell what pattern should be sewn into the sections.

_____ I'll write a **FANTASY STORY** about a magic quilt that carries sleepers off in dreams to the place the quilt tells about.

_____ I'll write a **DESCRIPTIVE PARAGRAPH** of a modern quilt that would tell about life today.

◄|WRITE|►

Use the lines below to plan your caption, story, or description. You may also want to use art materials to illustrate your writing.

_____

_____

_____

_____

_____

_____

_____

_____

_____

_____

◄|A SUGGESTION FOR SHARING|►

With a partner, go over your drafts and any drawings you've made. Talk about what you like in your drafts. On the lines below, jot some ideas you got from your partner's work. Then make a final copy of your own work.

_____

_____

_____

_____

GOING ON

If you liked writing about patterns, you might also enjoy writing about patterns found in caves (Activity 48).

Skeletons!

▲▲▲

Top Secret Photo From the Files of Dr. Fun E. Bonne

Why Did Dr. Bonne Make This Photo?

▼▼▼

◄| RESPOND |►

► There are six skeletons in the picture. To whom or what do they belong?

_____

_____

_____

_____

► How do you know which skeleton is which?

_____

_____

CHOOSE A FORM FOR YOUR WRITING

____ I'll write a **NEWSPAPER STORY** to go with the headline and to answer the question in it.

____ I'll write a **POEM** that tells how I feel about skeletons.

____ I'll choose one of the skeletons, find out more about it, and **DRAW AND LABEL** the parts of it in detail.

◄|WRITE|►

Use the lines below to plan your news story or your poem. If you're going to make a drawing, use the lines to note the labels you'll use on the drawing.

_____

_____

_____

_____

_____

_____

_____

_____

_____

_____

_____

◄|A SUGGESTION FOR REVISING|►

Get a partner's comments about the draft of your news story, poem, or labeled drawing. Write the most helpful suggestions below. Then use them as you write or draw your final version.

_____

_____

_____

_____

GOING ON

If you liked writing about mysterious skeletons, you might also like writing about a mysterious house (Activity 15).

Symbols

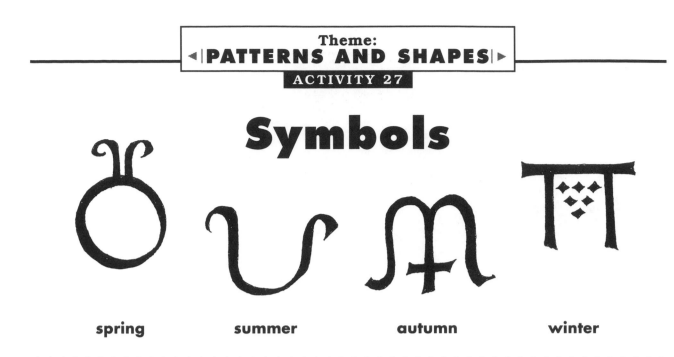

| spring | summer | autumn | winter |

▲▲▲▲▲▲▲▲▲▲▲▲▲▲▲▲▲▲▲▲▲▲▲▲▲▲▲▲▲▲▲▲▲▲▲▲▲▲▲

Symbols are signs, pictures, or things that stand for ideas. The symbols above date back to the Middle Ages in Europe, and were a sort of shorthand. Farmers used them in their record books. Writers used them in their journals.

Living things are symbols, too. Take birds, for example: Eagles are symbols of independence and courage. Doves symbolize peace, owls stand for wisdom, robins stand for springtime, and bluebirds for happiness. You probably know other animals that stand for strength, intelligence, slyness, timidity, and good luck.

In days gone by, some families had special symbols called a *coat of arms*. Pictures and colors in the coat of arms stood for things the family or individual valued. Below the coat of arms was a motto or saying that expressed a special belief or goal.

▼▼▼▼▼▼▼▼▼▼▼▼▼▼▼▼▼▼▼▼▼▼▼▼▼▼▼▼▼▼▼▼▼▼▼▼▼▼▼

◄| RESPOND |►

Name two or three nonliving symbols you see every day.

_____

_____

_____

CHOOSE A FORM FOR YOUR WRITING

____ I'll decide on an animal to be my special symbol. I'll **WRITE A PARAGRAPH TO EXPLAIN** why I chose this animal.

____ I'll use symbols in a **REBUS STORY** about myself.

____ I'll design my personal **COAT OF ARMS** and write a **MOTTO** to go with it.

(Activity 27 continued)

◄| **WRITE** |►

Use the lines below to plan your explanation or rebus. Use art materials and the back of this sheet to make your coat of arms.

_____

_____

_____

_____

_____

_____

_____

_____

_____

_____

_____

_____

_____

◄| **A SUGGESTION FOR SHARING** |►

When you've finished your work, get together with a group of classmates and discuss the symbols you've used. Talk about how the symbols help you learn more about one another.

GOING ON

If you liked exploring symbols, you might also enjoy writing about weather signs (Activity 34).

The Mystery of Moonrise

▲▲

You've seen this mystery. As the full moon rises over the horizon, it looks tremendous! Later in the night, when the moon is high above you, it looks much smaller. We know this is just an illusion. If you take photos of the moon in both positions and measure the diameter, it's exactly the same.

One scientific theory for the illusion is that at moonrise, we're comparing the size of the moon with buildings and trees on the horizon, so the moon looks bigger. But this theory doesn't always apply. The rising moon also looks larger far out at sea, and in planetariums where a moon image is projected on the edge of the dome. Another theory is that objects look smaller when we look at them with raised eyes, as we look at the moon later at night.

▼▼

◀| RESPOND |▶

Do you think it's important to solve the "mystery of moonrise"? Tell why or why not.

_____

_____

_____

_____

_____

_____

_____

CHOOSE A FORM FOR YOUR WRITING

___ I'll observe the full moon at four different times of the night and write a **REPORT** about my observations.

___ I'll devise a way, other than photos, of measuring the diameter of the full moon at different times of night. Then I'll write an **EXPLANATION** of my strategy.

___ I'll write a **POEM** about the full moon as it rises, moves across the sky, and sets.

(Activity 28 continued)

◄|WRITE|►

Use the lines below to draft your report, explanation, or poem.

_____

_____

_____

_____

_____

_____

_____

_____

_____

_____

_____

_____

_____

_____

_____

◄| A SUGGESTION FOR SHARING |►

Get together with a classmate who chose the same writing form you did. Discuss and compare your observations and ideas.

GOING ON

If you liked writing about the moon, you might also enjoy writing about a hollow earth (Activity 13).

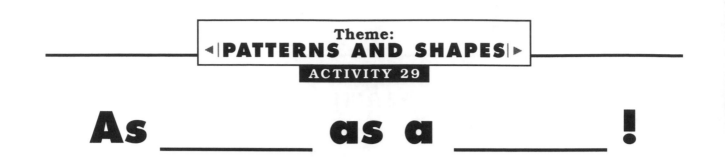
As _____ as a _____ !

▲▲

As bright as a new penny. As stubborn as a mule. As quiet as a mouse. When it comes to comparing things, the "as ___ a..." pattern turns up a lot in old sayings!

Many of the "as ___ a..." comparisons, like the ones above, are easy to understand. A new penny *is* bright, a mule *can* be stubborn, and a mouse *is* quiet. Some other "as ___ a...." comparisons may be a little harder to understand. For example, what does it mean when you say someone is "as independent as a hog on ice"? You'd have to know that a hog can't walk on ice very well (who can?), and so it isn't independent at all! Some other old "as ___ a..." comparisons are as follows:

as easy as pie;   as right as rain;   as cute as a bug's ear;

as smart as forty crickets; as sick as a cat;   as slick as a whistle;

as long as a country mile.

Comparisons like these are in use today because they're fun to say, even if we don't always understand what they mean!

▼▼

◄│ RESPOND │►

Note a couple of old "as ___ a..." comparisons that *you've* heard a lot.

_____

_____

_____

_____

_____

(Activity 29 continued)

CHOOSE A FORM FOR YOUR WRITING

___ I'll choose two or three of the puzzling comparisons and write an **EXPLANATION** of what I think they mean.

___ I'll list several other "as a..." comparisons used in my family and neighborhood, and use them to make an **OLD SAYINGS GLOSSARY.**

___ I'll write a **FABLE** that gives a make-believe story of how one of the "as a..." comparisons came to be.

◄ WRITE ►

Use the lines below to draft your explanation, glossary, or fable.

_____

_____

_____

_____

_____

_____

_____

_____

_____

_____

_____

_____

_____

◄ A SUGGESTION FOR REVISING ►

Your explanation, glossary, or fable might be clearer to your readers if you accompany it with one or more illustrations to further show a comparison's meaning. Show your draft to a partner and ask where illustrations would be helpful. Then make the illustrations yourself or ask your partner to help you with them.

GOING ON

If you liked writing about old sayings, you might also enjoy writing about beautiful sounds (Activity 21).

✳ A SPECIAL FORM: *A Collage*

▲▲

A collage is an artwork made by pasting materials onto a background to form an intriguing picture or pattern. Many collages have a theme or central idea, such as symbols, skeletons, or illusions; or love, hope, or fear; or home, friendship, or travel.

The main material in most collages is bits and pieces of paper that have on them parts of pictures, whole sentences or parts of sentences, and single words. Collage artists clip most of these from magazines or newspapers, sometimes adding a few words, sentences, or pictures of their own.

On your own or with a partner, you can make a collage that tells about a theme or idea that interests you. Keep the end result in mind: when viewers see your collage, they should be able to guess the theme or idea, even though it's not stated directly.

▼▼▼

Follow the steps on this page and the next to make your collage.

1. Brainstorm some themes you'd like to develop in a collage.

_____

_____

2. Go through the magazines, newspapers, and other materials your teacher has provided to find pictures, words, and phrases that relate to your themes. Then circle the theme above, for which you think you can find the most materials for your collage. Write your theme here:

_____

3. Get together the materials you'll need to make your collage

- a large sheet of oaktag for backing
- paste or glue
- pencil, eraser, pen
- scissors
- colored markers

Also gather the magazines, newspapers, and other materials from which you'll cut the pictures and words to use in your collage.

4. Cut out the words and pictures you want to use to develop your theme. In the long run, you may not be able to use all of them, but it's best to start with a lot. In the space below, draw a miniature version of where you'd like each collage piece to go.

5. Now arrange your collage pieces on the oaktag backing. If all the parts won't fit, decide which ones you'll discard, and why.

When you're satisfied with the pattern, paste the pieces to the backing.

6. Use your markers to outline key parts of your collage or to write in words or sayings that build the collage theme.

7. Now you've created an artwork whose pictures and patterns, words and sentences express something important to you. Display your collage and invite your classmates to discuss it. Can they guess the theme or general idea? What particular parts of the collage helped them reach their conclusion?

_____

_____

_____

Theme:
◄| FACT AND FICTION |►

Who's Doing What

ACTIVITY 31	**Newspaper Article**	**Opinion Paragraph**	**Humorous Story**	**Other Forms**
ACTIVITY 32	**Question List**	**Fiction Story**	**Retelling a Legend**	**Other Forms**
ACTIVITY 33	**Survey Form**	**Poem**	**Legend**	**Other Forms**
ACTIVITY 34	**Research Report**	**Weather Log**	**Illustrated Booklet**	**Other Forms**
ACTIVITY 35	**Science Report**	**Pictures and Captions**	**Fantasy Story**	**Other Forms**

Help! I'm a Prisoner in a UFO!

▲▲

Every once in a while, you hear or read a story about someone who says she or he was captured by beings from outer space and taken aboard their saucer-shaped spacecraft. After undergoing strange tests, the earthling is set free and reports the story to the newspapers.

Some people believe these stories. They figure that there must be other civilizations in the universe that are curious about our planet and want to come here to check things out. On the other hand, many people don't believe the stories at all. To them, the photos of flying saucers look like frisbees or pot lids or the whirl of a flashlight beam. The argument between believers and nonbelievers goes on and on.

▼▼

◄| RESPOND |►

Do you believe UFO stories? What's your main reason for believing or not believing them?

_____

_____

_____

_____

_____

_____

_____

_____

CHOOSE A FORM FOR YOUR WRITING

____ I'll imagine I'm a newspaper reporter and write an **ARTICLE** about someone who claims to have escaped from a UFO.

____ I'll write some paragraphs expressing and backing up my **OPINION** about UFO stories.

____ I'll imagine I was captured by creatures from a UFO and write a **HUMOROUS STORY** about my adventure.

◄| **WRITE** |►

Use the lines below to draft your article, opinion paragraphs, or story.

_____

_____

_____

_____

_____

_____

_____

_____

_____

_____

_____

_____

_____

◄| **A SUGGESTION FOR REVISING** |►

Articles, opinions, and stories are most enjoyable to read when they have an understandable sequence. Exchange drafts with a writing partner, read carefully for sequence, and then suggest ways the sequence might be made clearer. Use your partner's best suggestions when you write your final draft.

GOING ON

If you liked writing about peculiar sights in the sky, you might also enjoy writing about moonrise (Activity 28).

It Happened to My Friend's Friend's Friend

▲▲▲▲▲▲▲▲▲▲▲▲▲▲▲▲▲▲▲▲▲▲▲▲▲▲▲▲▲▲▲▲▲▲▲▲▲▲▲

Here's the story: An ordinary person is driving along a highway and spots a limousine with a flat tire stranded at the side of the road. The driver gets out to help and finds that the limousine belongs to a famous star, like Madonna or Arnold Schwarzenegger. The driver changes the tire for the famous star, is deeply thanked, and often receives a reward in the mail, such as free tickets to a big concert.

This story is told often, by many different people, and stars many different celebrities. The storyteller believes it's true, and usually begins by saying something like, "This didn't happen to me, but it happened to a friend of a friend of my uncle's." Familiar stories that begin that way are called "modern legends." There are hundreds of such legends. Have you heard the one about the woman who bought an expensive sports car for just $50 because...? (This happened to a friend of a friend of my cousin's friend!)

▼▼▼▼▼▼▼▼▼▼▼▼▼▼▼▼▼▼▼▼▼▼▼▼▼▼▼▼▼▼▼▼▼▼▼▼▼▼▼

◄| RESPOND |►

► How do you think a modern legend gets started?

_____

_____

► How do you think a modern legend travels?

_____

_____

CHOOSE A FORM FOR YOUR WRITING

____ I'll write a **LIST OF QUESTIONS** to use to check out whether a "friend of a friend of a friend" story is true.

____ I'll imagine the "stranded movie star" legend is true, and write a **STORY** explaining where the star was going and why she or he couldn't change the tire.

____ I'll write a **RETELLING** of a modern legend I've heard.

(Activity 32 continued)

◀ | WRITE | ▶

Use the lines below to draft your list, story, or retelling of a legend.

_____

_____

_____

_____

_____

_____

_____

_____

_____

_____

_____

_____

_____

_____

_____

◀ | A SUGGESTION FOR SHARING | ▶

Writers of stories and retellings can get together with classmates who wrote "check-the-story" questions. Present the stories and retellings aloud. Then answer the interviewer's questions.

GOING ON

If you liked writing about modern legends, you might also like writing about old ones (Activity 9).

Superstitious? Not Me!

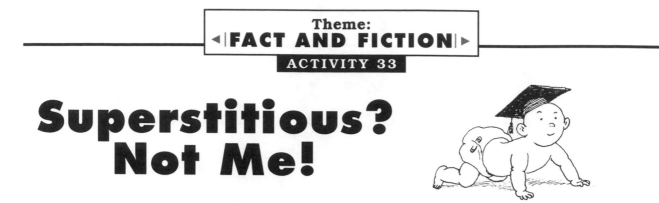

▲▲▲

A superstition is a belief founded on fear or on a mistaken belief. Here are some superstitions from different parts of the world:

It's bad luck if...a black cat crosses your path; you walk under a ladder; you step on a crack; you rock an empty chair; there are 13 guests at your party; you put a hat on a bed.

It's good luck if...a squirrel crosses your path; you look at the new moon over your left shoulder; you make a wish when you see a white horse or a load of hay; you eat peas on New Year's Day.

Many superstitions are about predictions and cures:

Bald-headed babies will be good students.

If you drop a fork, you'll soon have a fight.

To get rid of warts, tie knots in a string for each wart. Then bury the string.

We up-to-date people usually think we're not superstitious. But that's not always so. For example, many modern-day athletes have superstitions. Some baseball players think it's bad luck if a dog walks across the diamond before the first pitch. Some bowlers think that if you're on a winning streak, you should wear the same clothes. Some golfers carry coins in their pockets for good luck.

▼▼▼

◄| RESPOND |►

What's a superstition you've heard a lot? Does it affect *your* feelings and behavior? Tell why or why not.

_____

_____

_____

(Activity 33 continued)

CHOOSE A FORM FOR YOUR WRITING

____ I'll write a **SURVEY FORM** and interview people to find out what superstitions they believe in.

____ I'll write a **POEM** about superstitions.

____ I'll write a how-it-happened **LEGEND** to tell how a certain superstition started.

◄|WRITE|►

Use the lines below to draft your survey form, poem, or legend.

_____

_____

_____

_____

_____

_____

_____

_____

_____

_____

_____

_____

_____

_____

_____

_____

_____

◄| A SUGGESTION FOR REVISING |►

In England, there's a superstition that if you step gently on your school book, you'll get all your lessons right, including spelling! Think of a nonsuperstitious way to check the spelling in your survey form, poem, or legend. Then use that strategy.

GOING ON

If you liked writing about ancient beliefs, you might also enjoy writing about an ancient land (Activity 17).

Weather Wizards

▲▲

TV weather reporters use maps, satellite photos, radar, and weather bureau data to forecast the weather. But farmers and sailors have been doing accurate forecasts for centuries, and without all the modern gadgets. Many of these forecasts are based on accurate observations about the natural world, and come down to us in the form of rhymes and sayings. Here's one you've probably heard:

> Red sky at night is a sailor's delight.
> Red sky at morning, sailors take warning.

Meterologists (weather scientists) say this forecast is usually accurate, and that the following ones are, too.

> When the dew is on the grass
> Rain today won't come to pass.
> Sound traveling far and wide
> A stormy day will betide.

Of course, some old weather forecasts don't hold up. It's not true that "if onion skins are thick, the winter will be harsh," or that "if a cat washes behind its ears, a storm is coming."

▼▼▼

◄| RESPOND |►

Why do you think weather forecasting has always been important to farmers and sailors?

_____

_____

_____

CHOOSE A FORM FOR YOUR WRITING

___ I'll do research to find out why one of the old accurate forecasts is accurate, and write a **REPORT** about it.

___ I'll use my senses and observation skills to make weather predictions for a week, and write my predictions in a **LOG.**

___ I'll collect old weather sayings by interviewing people and then make an **ILLUSTRATED BOOKLET** on the subject.

◄ WRITE ►

Use the lines below to plan your report, log, or booklet.

_____

_____

_____

_____

_____

_____

_____

_____

_____

_____

_____

_____

_____

_____

◄ A SUGGESTION FOR REVISING ►

Your readers will want to know the sources of your information. For example, what books did you use to discover why an old forecast is accurate? What senses did you use to make weather predictions? Whom did you interview to collect more weather sayings? Write a list of your sources to include at the end of your piece of writing.

GOING ON

If you liked writing about weather patterns, you might also enjoy writing about another kind of pattern (Activity 25).

Birds on the Moon

▲▲▲

Where do many kinds of birds go as cold weather moves in? About 400 years ago, many people believed that certain birds spent the winter on the moon! After all, on clear, frosty autumn nights you could see huge flocks of birds flying high in the sky toward that shining globe. A hundred years later, few people believed this anymore. Now it was thought that birds actually spent the winter at the bottom of lakes and ponds, as frogs and turtles do. Some birds, it was believed, stayed at the bottom of the ocean till spring returned. It seemed like a sensible theory at the time: flocks of birds were seen flying out over the ocean in the fall, and coming back from the same direction in the spring.

Now that we know about bird migration, it's easy to laugh at these ancient ideas about birds. Here's another one: For a long time, some people thought screech owls brought tiny blind snakes back to their nests alive, and kept them there to eat up the grubs and other junk that piled up in the nest. But this "ancient idea" has turned out to be absolutely true!

▼▼▼

◄| RESPOND |►

In science, do ideas about what's "absolutely true" sometimes change? Explain why or why not.

_____

_____

_____

(Activity 35 continued)

CHOOSE A FORM FOR YOUR WRITING

____ I'll research what birds in my area migrate and write a **REPORT** about it.

____ I'll do some research about birds and find some "astounding-but-true" facts about them to **ILLUSTRATE** and **CAPTION.**

____ I'll write a **FANTASY STORY** about birds going to the moon.

◄| WRITE |►

Use the lines below to draft your report, captions, or story.

_____

_____

_____

_____

_____

_____

_____

_____

_____

_____

_____

_____

◄| A SUGGESTION FOR REVISING |►

All forms of writing benefit from exact and colorful verbs and descriptive words. Exchange your draft with a partner who chose a writing form different from yours. Help one another replace ho-hum words with rich and accurate ones.

GOING ON

If you liked writing about amazing birds, you might also enjoy writing about an amazing bear (Activity 3).

✳

A SPECIAL FORM:
A Fact-and-Fiction Map

▲▲▲

Many hundreds of years ago, mapmakers drew and illustrated maps on the basis of what explorers and travelers told them. Some of the stories were accurate. Others were based on misunderstandings or on a vivid imagination. As a result, many of these ancient maps consist of both fact and fiction. For example, some rivers and mountains might be shown accurately, while others were in the wrong place, or didn't exist at all. Pictures and captions on the map might show real cities and real people at work, but they might also show flying lions, three-headed humans, or trees with golden apples.

On your own or with a partner, you can make your own fact-and-fiction map. Think of the end result as a game: your classmates will study your map and try to tell which pictures and information on it are fiction and which are factual.

▼▼▼

Follow the steps on this page and on the next page.

1. Decide which country you'll show on your map.

_____

2. Make up a new name for the country.

_____

3. In the space to the right, draw or trace the outline of the country. (Later, you'll make a larger outline on a large sheet of paper.)

4. Research the country you've chosen to find several amazing-but-true facts about it. (The more amazing they are, the more fun your classmates will have trying to determine if they're true!) Try to include facts about people, animals, places, weather, history, and land and water forms. List some of your amazing-but-true facts.

_____

_____

_____

_____

_____

5. Now make up some amazing-but-untrue statements about the country.

_____

_____

_____

_____

_____

6. Get together the materials you'll need for your final product:
- a large sheet of heavy drawing paper;
- materials for drawing, writing, and painting.

7. Illustrate your map with your factual and fictional details. Write an interesting caption for each one.

8. Present your map to your classmates. Challenge them to find out which details show fiction and which show fact. As part of this challenge, ask your classmates to decide what *real* country your map outline and facts represent.

9. Put all the maps in a big folder. Use the maps to get ideas for stories, poems, and reports.

Theme:
◄|HEROES AND HEROINES|►

Who's Doing What

ACTIVITY 37	List	Description	Letter	Other Forms
ACTIVITY 38	Dialogue	Character Sketch	Survey Questions	Other Forms
ACTIVITY 39	Calendar	Fantasy Story	Story Summary	Other Forms
ACTIVITY 40	Play Script	Opinion Paragraphs	Essay	Other Forms
ACTIVITY 41	Biography	Autobiography	Character Sketch	Other Forms

So You Want to Be King!

▲▲▲

People usually like to know that their leaders are in good health. Our president goes jogging to show that he's physically fit to tackle the big job of leading the country. But in olden days, many leaders had to prove their physical fitness in more extreme ways. Here are some tasks that the *pharaohs,* or leaders of ancient Egypt had to perform to keep their jobs:

- run a race around markers that stood for the borders of the kingdom;
- display skill at killing lions;
- shoot an arrow through a thick sheet of copper;
- win difficult wrestling contests.

▼▼▼

◀▮ RESPOND ▮▶

Are physical skills important for leaders today? Tell why or why not.

_____

_____

_____

_____

CHOOSE A FORM FOR YOUR WRITING

____ I'll write a **LIST** of qualities and skills that a leader today should have.

____ I'll imagine and **DESCRIBE** some physical contests for leaders today.

____ I'll pretend I'm a pharaoh and write a **LETTER** to my family describing the physical contests I had to go through.

◄ | **WRITE** | ►

Use the lines below to draft your list, description, or letter.

_____

_____

_____

_____

_____

_____

_____

_____

_____

_____

◄ | **A SUGGESTION FOR SHARING** | ►

Get together with a classmate who chose the same writing form you did. Compare and discuss your ideas. Then fill out this chart.

My Best Ideas:

My Partner's Best Ideas:

GOING ON

If you liked writing about contests, you might also enjoy writing about a test for clowns (Activity 8).

Wonder Woman!

▲▲▲

*W*onder Woman comics began about 50 years ago. In these comics, Wonder Woman was really the goddess Diana from ancient times. Her mother instructed her to go to earth and help solve big problems. No way could Diana fly around earth looking like an ancient goddess! So she took on an everyday form and went to work on a newspaper, where she was known as Diana Prince. But secretly, when troubles hit the city, Diana put on her Wonder Woman clothes and went zooming about to defeat the bad guys and restore order.

▼▼

◄┃ RESPOND ┃►

Who is your favorite comic book hero or heroine? Why do you admire this person?

_____

_____

_____

_____

_____

CHOOSE A FORM
FOR YOUR WRITING

___ I'll **DRAW** a comic strip and **WRITE THE DIALOGUE** for my favorite comic strip heroine or hero.

___ I'll make up a whole new comic strip hero or heroine and write a **CHARACTER SKETCH** to describe this person.

___ I'll write questions for a **SURVEY** to find out what my classmates think a hero or heroine should be like.

(Activity 38 continued)

◄|WRITE|►

Use the lines below to draft your comic strip dialogue, your description, or the questions for your survey.

_____

_____

_____

_____

_____

_____

_____

_____

_____

_____

_____

_____

_____

◄| A SUGGESTION FOR REVISING |►

Work with a writing partner to check out the spelling, punctuation, and handwriting on your draft. Whether you've written comic-strip words, a character sketch, or survey questions, your writing has to be clear to your audience!

GOING ON

If you liked writing about the chores of super heroes and super heroines, you might also enjoy writing about the chores of a real-life person (Activity 10).

The 1,001 Tales of Scheherezade

▲▲▲

What a curious and cruel ruler was the Sultan Shahriyar! He looked for a wife who could entertain him all night with wonderful stories. If a woman failed to do this, he had her killed at daybreak. But the amazing Scheherazade more than passed the test.

For a thousand-and-one nights, she told the sultan incredible tales, each one different, and each one more marvelous than the last. The sultan was so impressed that he married her and gave her great riches. But more important to Scheherazade was the fact that her tales were written down so that people everywhere could enjoy them always. Her stories are known as *The Arabian Nights*.

▼▼▼

◀| RESPOND |▶

▶ Do you think you could make up 1,001 different stories?

_____

▶ Would your answer change if your life depended on it?

_____

▶ Explain why or why not.

_____

_____

CHOOSE A FORM FOR YOUR WRITING

___ I'll make a **CALENDAR** showing 1,001 nights. I'll write a **CAPTION** telling how many months and years that is.

___ I'll make believe I'm Scheherazade and write a **STORY** that will entrance and interest the Sultan.

___ I'll find a collection of The *Arabian Nights* and write a **SUMMARY** of one of Scheherazade's stories.

(Activity 39 continued)

◄│WRITE│►

Use the lines below to figure out your calendar or to draft your story or summary.

_____

_____

_____

_____

_____

_____

_____

_____

_____

_____

_____

_____

_____

◄│A SUGGESTION FOR SHARING│►

If you made a calendar, post it on a bulletin board. Challenge your classmates to write on it a different story subject for each of the 1,001 days. If you wrote a story or a summary, tell the story aloud to your classmates.

GOING ON

If you liked writing about challenges, you might also like writing about a challenging job (Activity 7).

What's a Friend For, Anyway?

▲▲

There is an ancient Greek legend about the loyalty Greeks thought friends owed one another. It seems there were two young friends named Damon and Pythias. Both offended the terrible tyrant Dionysius, and Pythias was condemned to death. Pythias had a family at home in the Greek colony of Syracuse.

"Dionysius," begged Pythias. "Allow me to return home for just a while to settle my affairs with my wife and children. Then I swear to you I will return to be executed, as you have decreed."

Dionysius laughed. "Let's you, Damon, and I strike a bargain," he said. "If you're not back in a month, I shall execute your friend Damon in your place. Does this suit you, Damon?" Damon nodded. He trusted his friend, and knew he would honor promises and keep bargains.

Pythias returned to Syracuse and settled his business there. But his journey back to the land of Dionysius was filled with storms, monsters, and other dangers. Struggling on to free his friend Damon, Pythias arrived one day after the month was over, on the day of execution. "I am here," he said. "Release my friend and execute me, as was intended in the first place."

Dionysius was so amazed at the loyalty of these two friends that he set them both free.

▼▼

◀| RESPOND |▶

In your opinion, would most people have returned to the scene of their execution as Pythias did? Explain your answer.

_____

_____

(Activity 40 continued)

CHOOSE A FORM FOR YOUR WRITING

____ I'll write a short **PLAY SCRIPT** to tell the story of Damon and Pythias. I'll add details of my own to the script.

____ I'll write some **PARAGRAPHS** that give my **OPINION** about the bargain made by Dionysius, Pythias, and Damon.

____ I'll write an **ESSAY,** or collection of my thoughts, about what friends do and don't owe to one another.

◄|WRITE|►

Use the lines below to plan your play script, paragraphs of opinion, or essay.

_____

_____

_____

_____

_____

_____

_____

_____

_____

_____

_____

_____

◄| A SUGGESTION FOR SHARING |►

Get together with classmates who chose the same writing form you did. Exchange your drafts or plans and read to find likenesses and differences. Discuss them. Then use ideas from the discussion to help you revise your writing.

GOING ON

If you liked writing about two men who symbolize friendship, you might also enjoy exploring some other symbols (Activity 27).

The Story of Sarah Winnemucca

▲▲

We think of heroines and heroes as people who attain some great goal. For example, Sacajawea reached her goal of helping two Anglo explorers, Lewis and Clark, find a waterway passage to the Pacific Ocean. Pocahontas reached her goal of helping many Europeans understand and respect the ways of her people. People who reach their goals are usually praised and remembered. People who don't reach them are often forgotten.

Sarah Winnemucca didn't reach her goal. Sarah—whose Indian name was *Toc-me-to-ne*, or Shell Flower—was a Paiute Indian. Her goal was to restore Indian lands to Indians and to improve the living conditions of the Paiute and other Native Americans. In 1880, she met with President Hayes to protest the way the Paiute were being robbed of their land. She gave speeches from San Francisco to Boston to tell about how the Paiute were being mistreated. Though audiences praised her speeches, they offered no help. Discouraged and angry, Sarah Winnemucca retired from public life. She started two schools for Native American children in Washington and Nevada.

▼▼

◄| RESPOND |►

In your opinion, is Sarah Winnemucca a heroine? Give some reasons for your opinion.

_____

_____

_____

CHOOSE A FORM FOR YOUR WRITING

____ I'll do some research to find out more about Sarah Winnemucca. Then I'll write a brief **BIOGRAPHY** about her.

____ I'll write an **AUTOBIOGRAPHICAL** story about a time when I tried hard to reach a big goal, but failed.

____ I'll write a **CHARACTER SKETCH** about a person I know who is a heroine or hero to me, even though she or he isn't famous.

◄| WRITE |►

Use the lines below to plan your biography, autobiography, or character sketch.

_____

_____

_____

_____

_____

_____

_____

_____

_____

_____

_____

◄| A SUGGESTION FOR REVISING |►

Good biographies, autobiographies, and character sketches concentrate on the deeds and actions of a person, and on his or her motives and beliefs. Less attention is given to physical descriptions of the person. Read through your draft to make sure you've emphazised your subject's actions and the reasons behind these actions. Add more information about these things, if you think it will improve your piece of writing.

GOING ON

If you liked writing about real-life heroes and heroines, you might like writing about some who are unknown (Activity 11).

✳

A SPECIAL FORM:
A News Release

▲▲

Anews release or news bulletin tells about an exciting and important event that's just happened. Often, the story is about something wonderful that an individual has accomplished. The news release may appear in a newspaper or be read over television or radio.

Imagine that it's ten years or so from now and you have just accomplished something great that millions of people will want to know about. Write a news release about it. Here's an example:

> YOUNG SCIENTIST
> FINDS FOSSILS OF UNUSUAL DINOSAUR
>
> April 8, 2006
> For immediate release:
>
> Jannette Haro, a student paleontologist working in Utah, has just uncovered the fossilized bones of a dinosaur unknown until now. Haro's careful study of the fossils shows that the animal is a direct ancestor of the ostrich. This is a link that scientists have been trying to find for decades. Dr. Millicent Chang, Haro's supervisior, says, "Without Janette's keen observation and hard work, we might have missed these fossils completely." For her achievement, the young scientist will receive funds to continue her work, and the animal she discovered will be called the Harosaur.

▼▼

To plan your new release of the future, follow the steps on the next page.

1. Brainstorm a list of some great and newsworthy things that you dream of accomplishing in the next ten or fifteen years.

_____

_____

_____

_____

_____

_____

_____

2. Independently or with a partner, go over your list to decide on the accomplishment that could most likely become a reality for you. Write a headline to announce it.

_____

3. On a separate sheet of paper, write a draft of your news release of the future. Use the example on the opposite page as a form to follow.

4. Go over your draft with a writing partner to check spelling and punctuation. Also check to make sure you've given enough precise details to make your accomplishment clear to your readers.

5. Write your final copy. Maybe you'll want to accompany your news release with a picture, a map, or a graph.

◄ A SUGGESTION FOR SHARING ►

▶ You and your classmates can make a bulletin board display of your news releases, compile them in the form of a magazine, or copy them to make a "News of the Future" newspaper.

▶ Read and discuss the news releases with a small group of classmates. Talk about ways to reach the goals you've set in your news stories. For example, what strong skills do you have *now*? What skills will you have to build? How can you do it?

Theme:
◀|PUZZLING IT OUT|▶
Who's Doing What

ACTIVITY 43	Adventure Story	Riddle Collection	Riddle Poems	Other Forms
ACTIVITY 44	Game Directions	Puzzle Sentences	Dictionary Search	Other Forms
ACTIVITY 45	Animal Biography	Fiction Story	Description	Other Forms
ACTIVITY 46	Fiction Story	Journal Entry	Essay	Other Forms
ACTIVITY 47	Explanatory Paragraphs	Measurments Chart	Humorous Story	Other Forms
ACTIVITY 48	Hypothesis Paragraphs	Fiction Story	Description	Other Forms
ACTIVITY 49	Autobiography Story	Fantasy	Play Script	Other Forms

A Dangerous Riddle, and Some Safe Ones

▲▲▲

In the myths of ancient Greece, there was an amazing creature called the Sphinx. It had the head of a human, the body of a lion, and the wings of a bird. Perched angrily on a mountain top, the Sphinx asked a riddle to all travelers who passed by. Travelers couldn't come up with the right answer, and so the Sphinx ate them.

The riddle was "What moves first on four feet, then on two, and finally on three?" The Greek hero Oedipus, wandering by the hungry Sphinx, quickly unraveled the riddle. "The answer is *a human,*" he said. "For we crawl on all fours as babies, walk upright on two feet as adults, and use a cane when we are very old." Angry that the riddle was finally answered, the Sphinx killed itself.

Few riddles are taken as seriously as all this! Riddles today are for fun. Many riddles use wordplay, such as "Why don't doctors get angry?" Answer: Because they don't want to lose their patients (patience). Or "What has eyes but can't see?" (a potato). Today's riddlers may also set their riddles in the form of poems. Here's an example:

> A thin black snake filled with voices,
> I take your chatter in and out,
> Running from roof to road to roof.
> (a telephone wire)

▼▼▼

◄ RESPOND ►

Write the best riddle you've heard recently. Did the answer come as a surprise to you?

_____

_____

CHOOSE A FORM FOR YOUR WRITING

___ I'll write an **ADVENTURE STORY** about someone who had to solve a riddle or suffer a terrible fate!

___ I'll make a **COLLECTION OF RIDDLES** that are based on wordplay.

___ I'll write two or three **RIDDLE POEMS** that require readers to guess who the speaker is.

◄|WRITE|►

Use the lines below to draft your story or riddle poems. If you're collecting riddles based on wordplay, use a notebook or index cards to record your riddles.

_____

_____

_____

_____

_____

_____

_____

_____

_____

_____

_____

_____

_____

_____

◄|A SUGGESTION FOR REVISING|►

A riddle—whether it's mysterious or funny—has to be fair. That is, the clues in it have to make sense and add up in the long run. The person hearing the riddle has to be able to look back and say, "Oh, I see! All the clues were there. I just didn't pick up on them." With a writing partner, read your draft and make sure your riddles are "fair." Make any changes you think are necessary.

GOING ON

If you liked writing about riddles, you might also enjoy exploring anagrams (Activity 22).

What's a Word Worth?

▲▲▲

Some people say they don't like arithmetic. But most people say they *do* like word puzzles. So savvy puzzle makers often sneak arithmetic into word puzzles! In the example below, the letters of the alphabet are divided into sets, and each letter in that set is worth a number of points, or dollars.

$1	$2	$3	$4	$5
ABC	DEF	GHI	JKL	MNO

$6	$7	$8	$9
PQR	STU	VWX	YZ

Within a time frame, like one minute, players have to build words with a certain number of letters—say, 5 letters—to win as many dollars as they can. For example, *fable* is 2+1+1+4+2=$10, while *story* is 7+7+5+6+9=$34. With a six-letter challenge, players might come up with words like *report* (6+2+6+5+6+7=$32) or *legend* (4+2+3+2+5+2=$18). The winner is the player who earns the most word money within the time limit.

▼▼▼

◄| RESPOND |►

Some people are afraid of games that involve arithmetic. Why do you think this is so?

_____

_____

_____

_____

_____

_____

_____

CHOOSE A FORM FOR YOUR WRITING

___ I'll make up another word-and-number game and write **DIRECTIONS** for playing it.

___ I'll use the game above to write a $100 **SENTENCE** with as few words as possible.

___ I'll use a dictionary to find and **LIST 10 WORDS** that would add up to a whole lot of money for me, using the rules above.

(Activity 44 continued)

◄|**WRITE**|►

Use the lines below to plan your directions, sentence, or list.

.
_____

_____

_____

_____

_____

_____

_____

_____

_____

_____

_____

_____

_____

_____

_____

◄| **A SUGGESTION FOR REVISING** |►

People who make word puzzles have to be excellent spellers. Work with a partner and a dictionary to make sure you've spelled each and every word correctly in the first draft of your writing. Make any corrections that are necessary before you share your work with your classmates.

GOING ON

If you liked working with numbers, you might also enjoy doing some mouse math (Activity 5).

100-Word Animals

▲▲▲▲▲▲▲▲▲▲▲▲▲▲▲▲▲▲▲▲▲▲▲▲▲▲▲▲▲▲▲▲▲▲▲▲▲▲

Libraries are full of *Who's Who* books about famous humans. A man in North Carolina has started publishing a *Who's Who of Animals.* The animals don't have to be famous. They just have to be important to you. The animal can be a pet, like a dog, a cat, or a horse. Or it can be a wild animal, like a bird, a squirrel, a garter snake, a family of bats, or a chipmunk that you've gotten to know. Just send in a description by the deadline time, and your animal will be listed in the *Who's Who of Animals.*

But there's a catch! Your description of the animal has to be made in 100 words or less. With that small number of words, you try to capture the special qualities of the animal and why you love it. Here's a description, of less than 100 words, of a horse.

Sir Meadow Harvit
Cross Lanes, West Virginia

Sir was a 500-pound gelding owned, tamed, and trained by a 65-pound, 10-year-old girl who also sported a pony tail. He was a rambunctious rogue misunderstood by most, but in reality a gentle giant. While being brushed by his tiny owner, he would lay his head on her shoulder and nap. Christmas mornings were special for Sir. On that day his oats, apples, and carrots were heated on the family stove and lugged to the barn one small step at a time.

▼▼▼▼▼▼▼▼▼▼▼▼▼▼▼▼▼▼▼▼▼▼▼▼▼▼▼▼▼▼▼▼▼▼▼▼▼▼

◀ **RESPOND** ▶

Do you think it's a good idea to have a *Who's Who of Animals?* Explain your answer.

_____

_____

_____

_____

CHOOSE A FORM FOR YOUR WRITING

___ I'll use the form on the next page to write a 100-word **BIOGRAPHY** of a pet or other animal that I know well.

___ I'll use the description of Sir Meadow Harvit and his owner as an idea for a **STORY** about a girl and her horse.

___ I'll imagine that I have a very unusual pet, like an elephant, a dolphin, or a bat, and write a 100-word **DESCRIPTION** of this pet.

(Activity 45 continued)

◄| **WRITE** |►

Use the lines below to write your not-more-than-100-word description of a real or imaginary pet. If you're writing a story about the girl and her horse, write your draft on a separate sheet of paper.

Animal's full name _____

Hometown and State _____

Biography (100 words maximum)

_____

_____

_____

_____

_____

_____

_____

_____

◄| **SUGGESTIONS FOR REVISING** |►

► If you're writing a description of an animal, count the words in your first draft. Your limit is 100 words, so use them wisely. If your draft is over the limit, look for words and phrases you can take out without ruining the story. One strategy for doing this is to combine sentences. Here's an example

Draft: Rover was an excellent dog. He was good at catching Frisbees. He was also good at chasing squirrels. He was good at chasing cats, too. (25 words)

Revision: Rover was an excellent dog. He was good at catching Frisbees, and at chasing squirrels and cats. (17 words)

► If you chose to write a story about the horse and his owner, check your draft to make sure you've told how the girl and the horse feel about one another. Feelings make stories live and glow.

> **GOING ON**
> *If you liked describing animals, you might enjoy writing about a special dolphin (Activity 1).*

What's in a Name?

▲▲

Most of us keep the names our families gave us. But there have been lots of people who took new names when they grew up. Some writers have done it. Samuel Clemens renamed himself Mark Twain. Charles Dodgson used Lewis Carroll as his writing name. Some entertainers do it, too: Cherilyn Sarkesian is now just Cher and LaDonna Andrea Gaines is now Donna Summers.

Some people acquire strange nicknames that stick with them. Back in the 19th century, young Martha Jane Canary of Virginia City, Montana, grew up to be an expert horsewoman and sharpshooter. For a while, she

worked as a scout for the United States Army in Wyoming. Then, in 1878, she left that job to go to Deadwood, South Dakota. A smallpox epidemic had broken out there, and Martha became a heroine for nursing many victims of this awful disease back to health. Somewhere along the way, people began calling her Calamity Jane. But nobody knows *why* for sure. One story says that she once told some men that anyone who offended her would meet with a calamity. Another story says that she got the name when she responded to the calamity of the smallpox epidemic.

▼▼

◄| RESPOND |►

Imagine another reason why Martha Jane Canary became known as Calamity Jane.

_____

_____

_____

_____

CHOOSE A FORM FOR YOUR WRITING

____ I'll build on my response, and write a **FICTION STORY** about how Martha's nickname came to be.

____ I'll imagine myself as a hero or heroine who does a great deed and write a **JOURNAL ENTRY** telling how it won me a nickname.

____ I'll write an **ESSAY** giving several of my ideas about reasons some people change their names.

◄|WRITE|►

Use the lines below to draft your story, journal entry, or essay.

_____

_____

_____

_____

_____

_____

_____

_____

_____

_____

_____

_____

_____

_____

_____

_____

◄| A SUGGESTION FOR REVISING |►

Read your draft aloud to a writing partner. Then ask your partner to tell which parts are strongest and which need more work. Use some of your partner's ideas as your revise your writing.

GOING ON

If you liked writing about people's names, you might also enjoy writing about names of places (Activity 16).

Measure Me This!

▲▲▲

If you look around your classroom, you can probably quickly come up with several different standards for measuring things. For example, there are rulers and yardsticks for measuring length, clocks and watches for keeping track of minutes and hours, calendars for counting days and months, and thermometers for measuring temperatures.

But that's just the beginning! Almost everything you use has a special measurement standard. Light bulbs are measured in watts and lumens. (*Watts* are a measure of the electricity you'll pay for when you use the bulb, and *lumens* are a measure of the bulb's brightness.) Your pencils have a number on them, that is a measure of the lead's hardness. The food you eat is measured in calories. Paper is measured by a special kind of pound. The sizes of pins, paper clips, and rubber bands are indicated with special numbers.

Measuring doesn't stop with school. No matter what career you go into, there will be certain kinds of measurement standards and terms you'll learn to use. Ask any doctor, or farmer, or builder, or computer engineer, or auto designer, or pilot, or...

▼▼▼

◄ RESPOND ►

What's the value in knowing how to measure things?

_____

_____

_____

_____

CHOOSE A FORM FOR YOUR WRITING

___ I'll identify the career I'd like to have and write some paragraphs to **EXPLAIN** some measurements I'll have to use.

___ I'll research ways of measuring several different things, such as eggs, gold, radio waves, ships, and blood pressure. I'll organize my findings in a **CHART** or other visual device.

___ I'll write a **HUMOROUS STORY** about someone who tried to measure something with the wrong kind of tool.

◀|**WRITE**|▶

Use the lines below to draft your explanation or story, or to make notes for the chart you'll design.

_____

_____

_____

_____

_____

_____

_____

_____

_____

_____

_____

_____

◀|**A SUGGESTION FOR REVISING**|▶

When it comes to measurements, even one small mistake can throw a job off or result in a much bigger mistake. So proofread your writing or your chart two or three times to make sure the numbers you've written are absolutely correct.

GOING ON

If you enjoy measuring things, you might enjoy figuring out a way to measure friendship (Activity 40).

The Mystery of the Cave Paintings

▲▲▲

As long as there have been human beings, there has probably been art. For example, many paintings in caves in France and Spain date back more than 20,000 years. There's no mystery about the age of the paintings, because scientists use a method called radiocarbon analysis to date the charcoal used to make the paintings. There's no mystery about what the paintings show, either. They are vivid pictures of animals that abounded in Europe at that time. The artists showed bison, horses, and deer, as well as ibexes and chamois. In caves near the sea, there are paintings of seals, squid, fish, and jellyfish.

But there *are* at least two mysteries. One mystery is, why are there so many tracings of human hands over, around, and above the painted animals? What did these tracings stand for? Another mystery is who made the paintings, and why? One guess is that hunters made them to brag about the animals they'd hunted and killed. Another guess is that priests or priestesses made them *before* the hunt, to bring good luck to the hunters. A third guess is that teachers made them as they told children about the habits of animals in their environment.

▼▼▼

◄| RESPOND |►

Which "mystery" interests you more—the tracings of hands, or the mystery of who made the paintings and why?

_____

_____

(Activity 48 continued)

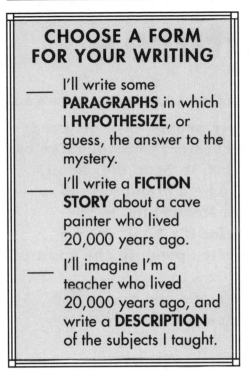

CHOOSE A FORM FOR YOUR WRITING

_____ I'll write some **PARAGRAPHS** in which I **HYPOTHESIZE**, or guess, the answer to the mystery.

_____ I'll write a **FICTION STORY** about a cave painter who lived 20,000 years ago.

_____ I'll imagine I'm a teacher who lived 20,000 years ago, and write a **DESCRIPTION** of the subjects I taught.

◀|WRITE|▶

Use the lines below to draft your hypothesis, story, or description.

_____

_____

_____

_____

_____

_____

_____

_____

_____

_____

_____

_____

_____

◀|A SUGGESTION FOR SHARING|▶

Get together with some classmates who chose the same writing form you did. Read your work aloud and discuss the likenesses and differences in your hypotheses, stories, or descriptions.

GOING ON

If you liked writing about the mystery of cave paintings, you might also enjoy writing about the mystery of words (Activity 19).

Mystery Creatures

▲▲

All over the world, and down through time, many people have believed in strange beings who appear now and then to ordinary humans like us. Even today, there are people who wait by Loch Ness, in Scotland, hoping to catch a glimpse of Nessie. Nessie is supposed to be a prehistoric, sea-serpent-like creature trapped in this ancient lake. Meanwhile, in the Himalaya mountains of Asia, other people search for Big Foot, a lumbering, kindly giant whose footprints supposedly appear in the snow of those high and windy peaks.

In Europe, people once believed in gnomes and trolls and pixies and leprechauns. Gnomes guarded treasures on hillsides. Trolls were nasty fellows who lived under bridges and in caves. Pixies and leprechauns played silly tricks on people. There were mysterious little people in Hawaii, too. They were known as *menehunes*, and they spent their nights building mysterious roads and bridges. In the Middle East, there were *jinns*, or genies, who lived in bottles and granted wishes to people who released them. Of course, we modern people don't believe in such things. (But don't tell that to the Tooth Fairy, the Easter Bunny, the Sand Man, or Jack Frost!)

▼▼

◄│ **RESPOND** │►

Why do you think so many people have believed in strange, mysterious creatures?

_____

_____

_____

CHOOSE A FORM FOR YOUR WRITING

____ I'll write an **AUTOBIOGRAPHICAL STORY** about an imaginary being I believed in when I was younger.

____ I'll write a **FANTASY STORY** about one of the creatures I've just read about.

____ I'll write a **PLAY SCRIPT** about a modern person who doesn't believe in imaginary creatures, but suddenly meets one!

◄| WRITE |►

Use the lines below to plan your story or script.

_____

_____

_____

_____

_____

_____

_____

_____

_____

_____

_____

_____

_____

◄| A SUGGESTION FOR REVISING |►

Get together with a classmate who chose the same writing form you did. As you read and talk about your drafts, focus on *sequence*. Help one another fill in any steps that seem to be missing.

GOING ON

If you liked writing about puzzling, mysterious, scary things, you might also enjoy writing about fears (Activity 20).

✳

A SPECIAL FORM:
A Writer's Book of Questions

▲▲▲

Some of the best stories in the world begin with a writer's question. In fact, you may be able to identify the stories that grew out of these questions that writers asked themselves:

- **What would happen if a pig made friends with a spider?**

- **What would happen if a girl had to live alone on an island for many years?**

- **What would happen if a toy rabbit wanted to become real?**

   With a group of classmates, you can begin and add to *A Book of Questions for Writers.* This book can be a source of ideas for you and other writers. On those murky ho-hum days when you're saying to yourself, "But there's nothing to write about," you can turn to the Question Book and turn on your idea factory!

▼▼▼

Here are some steps to practice and follow to build your *Book of Questions.*

1. Brainstorm together for themes or general subjects. Examples are **Stars**, **Automobiles**, **Television**, **Cold Weather**, **Oceans**. Write each theme on a separate page for your book.

2. Now brainstorm some questions about each theme. Your questions can be sensible and scientific, or extremely far-out. For example, under the theme *Stars*, you might ask, "What's a star made of?" or "What would happen if a distant star fell toward earth?" or "What would happen if a star wanted to be a movie star?"

Practice this strategy now by choosing another of the themes mentioned, and brainstorming several "What ...?" questions about it.

Theme:

_____

Questions:

_____

_____

_____

_____

Now discuss some writing ideas you get from these questions.

3. Make a folder to hold the pages of your *Book of Questions*. You'll probably need plenty of extra pages as you think of new themes, and of new questions for old themes. Put your *Book of Questions* on a table where it will be handy.

4. Use the *Book of Questions* to get ideas for your writing. Write in any form you choose—a poem, a folktale, a funny story, a report, a journal entry, a map, a sci-fi story, a play, a news report, whatever! Put the final draft of your piece of writing in the theme section where it belongs.

5. Plan ways to enjoy your finished pieces of writing together. One way is to have a Theme Day. When one section is chock-full of writing, work with your teacher to plan a time when you can read, show, or act out your work. On the lines below, write some other ideas for sharing the writing in your *Book of Questions*.

_____

_____

_____

_____

_____